"*Formed to Lead* challenges the conventional pursuit of leadership, inviting us instead to embrace the deeper invitation of Christ. Grounded in Scripture and rich with practical insight, this transformative guide reminds us that leadership is not about striving but surrender—recognizing that the work is the Lord's and true effectiveness flows from intimacy with him. When leadership becomes an overflow of the Spirit within us, we experience a profound unburdening anchored in the integrity of our true identity and purpose."

Andrew Ginsberg, president of Operation Mobilization USA

"Jason Jensen understands—and exemplifies—the truth that our leadership can never outpace our formation. Through a masterful blend of Scripture, timeless wisdom from church history, personal authenticity, and practical, adaptable practices, *Formed to Lead* offers fresh hope and new imagination to leaders hungry for all God has for them—and those they serve."

Kara Powell, chief of leadership formation at Fuller Seminary and coauthor of *Future-Focused Church*

"Leaders ignore their inner lives at great peril. This rich book, rooted in the Gospel of Luke, takes readers on a pilgrimage of self-reflection and spiritual formation. It explores—through a variety of church traditions—how building integrity, humility, and discernment fosters both personal centeredness and spiritual authority."

Alec Hill, president emeritus of InterVarsity Christian Fellowship/USA

"In a world where spiritual formation and character are often divorced from leadership, this book is timely. Filled with practical exercises and prayers, and grounded in Scripture and decades of experience, Jason Jensen's book invites us on a rich journey of formation—to reflect, listen, and discern. A must-read for any leader wanting to grow in his or her own discipleship and intimacy with God!"

Tom Lin, president and CEO of InterVarsity Christian Fellowship/USA

"Jason Jensen's life and leadership are marked by attentiveness to Scripture and spiritual disciplines, prayer and people, sabbath and sacrament. The pages of *Formed to Lead* are rich in wisdom and uncommonly practical application borne out of that sustained attentiveness. Enter into these pages, engage in the practices, and prayerfully apply what you encounter to your own leadership and spiritual formation."

Jeff Crosby, author of *The Language of the Soul* and *World of Wonders*

FORMED
to LEAD

HUMILITY

CHARACTER

INTEGRITY

—— and ——

DISCERNMENT

Jason Jensen

ĩvp

An imprint of InterVarsity Press
Downers Grove, Illinois

InterVarsity Press
P.O. Box 1400 | Downers Grove, IL 60515-1426
ivpress.com | email@ivpress.com

InterVarsity Press® is the publishing division of InterVarsity Christian Fellowship/USA®. For more information, visit intervarsity.org.

All Scripture quotations, unless otherwise indicated, are taken from The Holy Bible, New International Version®, NIV®. Copyright © 1973, 1978, 1984, 2011 by Biblica, Inc.™ Used by permission of Zondervan. All rights reserved worldwide. www.zondervan.com. The "NIV" and "New International Version" are trademarks registered in the United States Patent and Trademark Office by Biblica, Inc.™

While any stories in this book are true, some names and identifying information may have been changed to protect the privacy of individuals.

Figure 4.1. Photo of the Baptism Icon appears courtesy of Sharon Henthorn-Iwane. Used with permission.

Figure 7.1. El Camino de Santiago marker photo by Ángela Vázquez Fernández, CC BY-SA 4.0, via Wikimedia Commons

Figure 8.2. Labyrinth by Nordisk familjebok; vector: Sebastián Asegurado, public domain, via Wikimedia Commons

The publisher cannot verify the accuracy or functionality of website URLs used in this book beyond the date of publication.

Cover design: Faceout Studio, Spencer Fuller
Interior design: Jeanna Wiggins

ISBN 978-1-5140-0990-1 (print) | ISBN 978-1-5140-0991-8 (digital)

Printed in the United States of America ∞

Library of Congress Cataloging-in-Publication Data
A catalog record for this book is available from the Library of Congress.

31 30 29 28 27 26 25 | 13 12 11 10 9 8 7 6 5 4 3 2 1

FOR ABBY AND GABE

Because I love you with my whole heart,

I pray that God will lead you on your own paths

of deep formation intertwined

with compelling calling.

CONTENTS

INTRODUCTION

Lᴇᴛ ᴍᴇ ʙᴇ ʜᴏɴᴇsᴛ. The state of Christian leadership does not look great these days, especially here in the United States. Nearly every week I hear about another leader being revealed as a failure, an abuser, or an embarrassment. When I hear these accounts, my gut tightens and my heart beats fast with a sense of dread. I then have three concurrent impulses.

First, I feel heart-rending sadness. I grieve the pain of the victims, the followers, or both. I also grieve the leader's brokenness and pain. Second, I feel judgmental: *How could they possibly have done that? Why did nobody stop them sooner? What were they thinking? Lord, why don't you call and send better leaders?* Third, even in the midst of my judgment, I feel identification with the failure and fear that I could do the same. Lord Jesus, have mercy.

Christian leadership can feel hopelessly broken.

Leaders in both Christian and secular spaces are all subject to the forces of evil and the fallibilities of human nature. Our brokenness and our everyday messiness may seem insurmountable. And yet there is hope, because the Holy Spirit is still at work in the journey of God's people.

My own journey is a testimony to the kindness and power of Jesus. Since 1980 I have felt a call to follow Jesus with my whole life and to give my life away for others. In the last forty-four years of intentional leadership, I've tried a lot of stuff! At every stage of my imperfect leadership journey, God has shown me tremendous mercy and generosity. In formation and leadership I have gone from overconfident self-assurance to devastating failure, from weakness and depression to redemption and joy, and back again. I've led in direct service, middle management, and executive leadership. I have failed a lot, learned a lot, and been hurt by others—a lot. I've experienced intractable problems and conflicts and times of exuberant fruitfulness. I have had lonely times and rich community. I have learned about my own identity and the world through experiences of cultural displacement and through leaders profoundly different from myself. I've been blessed with great bosses, difficult supervisors, and amazing mentors. Through many stages of life and leadership, God has consistently called me to major on growing in my own discipleship—in intimacy and character as well as mission.

SPIRITUAL FORMATION AND LEADERSHIP

This book is about spiritual formation and leadership. For followers of Jesus, those two subjects are inextricably tied together. Their connection offers us both invitation and challenge.

Spiritual formation invites us to leadership. In his book *Invitation to a Journey*, Dr. Robert Mulholland offers a simple definition: "Spiritual formation is a process of being formed in the image of Christ for the sake of others." Formation is a great metaphor for our growth as disciples of Jesus. As Christians, we are always being shaped, moment by moment, into the image of Jesus or into another image. This reality ought to stop us in our tracks. Each moment is an opportunity to become more—or less—like Jesus. The goal of spiritual formation is for our heart and soul and character to be shaped like Jesus. Our choices about how we act and relate allow us to participate in (or resist) God's sculpting plans.

Note the last part of Mulholland's definition: "for the sake of others." When we become more like Jesus, we are always sent like Jesus, as agents of his kingdom for the sake of others. So spiritual formation at its best compels us toward a kind of leadership that influences the world for the kingdom of God.

But Christian leadership also invites us to spiritual formation. When we follow Jesus, he calls us to influence the world, and in that

process he always intends to shape us as mature disciples. The telos or
end goal of God's plan is the bride of Christ (his church in the world)
fully prepared for marriage. This includes the evangelism and justice
needed to fill God's kingdom, and it also includes growing God's
people into maturity.

Jesus does not call people to burnout. He does not invite us to compromise our character or integrity for the sake of his mission. He does
not use leaders as means to an end. Rather, he invites us to become
more humble and faithful and whole as we lead. He wants us to
embody his heart and mind as we do his will.

This combination of formation and leadership draws us into a deep
journey of faith, believing that God wants to heal us *and* send us, grow
us *and* use us. Leaders are often tempted to hold on to one of those
impulses and let go of the other, but I'm inviting you: dare to insist on
both. Holding formation and leadership together captures the authentic essence of God's kingdom.

Simply put, the work of Christian leadership should be shaped like
the gospel of Jesus. The story, tone, and impact of our work is meant
to reflect the good news. But the character, heart, and mind of the
leader is also meant to reflect Jesus. The only way these two come together is when we give ourselves fully to the Holy Spirit's work of
shaping us in the image of Jesus and sending us in his name. This
challenges us to constant growth for the whole of our lives.

As you read this book, you will find that it weaves back and forth
between leadership and formation. The first chapter focuses most directly on leadership, introducing Luke's surprising vision of Christian
leadership and its contrast with worldly assumptions. The subsequent
chapters focus on how the Spirit and the Word shape our leadership,
as every element of discipleship growth is relevant to our callings. The
final chapters consider discernment, which I see as the core competency of Christian leadership. I'm not presenting you with a manual
to optimize your leadership efficiency, but rather with invitations and
signposts on a profound journey of growth and mission together.

SCRIPTURE AND PRAYER

You will notice that this book is filled with Scripture reflections, particularly from Luke 1–4. I have come to believe that the early chapters
of Luke offer leaders a template for growth. The gospel shows us a
pattern in Jesus' own formation and calling. As we inhabit this pattern,
the Holy Spirit shapes us in the image of Jesus, in line with the Scriptures, and toward the Spirit's work in the world. This, my friends, is a
great recipe for Christian leadership with integrity and resilience. A
close reading of Luke 1–4 reveals the Holy Spirit and the Word of God
as the principal agents of Jesus' formation and calling. The Spirit and
the Word can shape our leadership in the same ways.

You will also notice that each chapter begins with a brief prayer. I'm
regularly praying these for you, because I believe that only God can
form leaders of integrity, humility, character, and discernment. If you
are a leader approaching crisis in your private or public life, I believe
God can meet you in the midst of that crisis, for the sake of growth and
influence. If you are a reluctant leader, I hope God will encourage you
to greater faith and thriving influence. If you are an enthusiastic leader,
I'm praying that the way of Jesus will challenge your notions of leadership and invite you on a profound journey of growth and influence. I
pray for congruence between your spirituality and your influence, your
faith and your action. I pray for alignment between your message and
your means, your character and your contribution. I believe that the
music of your soul can match the dancing of your work.

HOW TO READ THIS BOOK

Read with your Bible open. Most of the chapters encourage a close
reading of at least one passage. Don't take my interpretations for
granted—engage the text yourself! Your careful study and reflection
will always bring greater insight and growth.

Do the exercises. Each chapter offers a spiritual exercise at the end.
These are intended to help you experience the Holy Spirit's formation
in your own life. Ideas don't transform people on their own. Often the

Spirit uses ideas and practices together to shape our souls more into the image of Jesus.

Read and discuss with a team. Leadership in the kingdom of God is always communal as well as individual. The Holy Spirit wants to form teams, churches, organizations, small groups, and institutions that embody leadership integrity. In my experience, the Spirit moves most powerfully in groups as we study Scripture together. For simplicity, I have included seven group sessions where a team can spend an hour in a combination of Bible study and discussion of the chapters. Each session covers a portion of the book that the group should read before meeting—see the table of contents. I've included a simple leader's guide at the end of the book to help you steer your team through the process.

A final note: The stages and elements presented in this book may seem sequential, but I find them repeating again and again. Spiritual formation is not a linear process. At its best, our formation as spiritual leaders is a spiral. The Holy Spirit leads us around and around familiar territory, but at the same time ever deeper in a certain direction. My prayer for you is that the Spirit will use this book to lead you on an ever-deepening, formative journey of leadership integrity.

LEADERSHIP INTEGRITY

Luke's Surprising Vision

Lord Jesus, when we look closely, we sense that leadership is full of temptations. Teach us to see ourselves and the world more clearly. Show us a path forward to grow as both humble disciples and faith-filled leaders. Deliver us from pride and fear. Empower us and direct us by your Spirit. Amen.

As a Christian, I'm often skeptical about leadership. I look at public figures admired for leadership excellence and I feel torn. On one hand I long for similar strength, brilliance, and accomplishment. I want to be effective and smart, and in control. On the other hand I feel vaguely repelled. Most public leaders don't reflect much of Christ's character. Any faith they have seems like a thin veneer, a colorful user interface over a morally bankrupt operating system.

For example, I love the boldness and innovation I often see from leaders in the tech industry. Their strategic and creative brilliance has transformed the world in profound ways. Some of them manage to generate wealth and influence that serves great causes. I want to lead boldly and innovate for God's kingdom! At the same time as I look closely at many (but not all) of these leaders from the perspective of character and spirituality, I don't want to emulate them. I often see arrogance, abuse, or addiction at the core. I seldom see compassion, humility, or authentic faith.

In contrast, I think of my friend and mentor Mary Anne Voelkel. Mary Anne and her husband, Jack, were missionaries in Colombia for thirty years, planting a student ministry and passing leadership along to local leaders. She also planted a fruitful prayer, healing, and evangelism ministry in the prisons of Medellin in the 1980s during very turbulent times.

In 1990, I had the honor of being Mary Anne's chauffer and assistant during a conference where she was leading a large prayer effort. What an amazing experience it was! The Holy Spirit moved powerfully among students. Like we see in the book of Acts, the drama included healing, deliverance, conversion, and worship—along with significant conflict and resistance.

As I accompanied Mary Anne through that week of intense eighteen- to twenty-hour days, I saw what I call leadership integrity. She was the same in public and in private. She was consistent in success and failure, when receiving affirmation and pushback. She showed the fruit of the Holy Spirit while she ministered in the gifts of the Holy Spirit. Somehow while she was serving, it was her affection for Jesus that always came forward. She was able to forgive others and ask forgiveness when needed. While I was excited by the drama of the ministry, I was most impressed by learning from a leader whose character seemed congruent with her contribution. Later in friendship with Mary Anne, I learned more about the suffering God used to form her and about the private spiritual disciplines that made her leadership integrity possible.

The world admires leadership for its brilliance, its strength, and its impact. All of these can be good and redemptive when applied toward the kingdom of God. But Christian leadership holds another vision as well: a vision of integrity where our methods and character and presence reflect the Spirit of Jesus. For Christian leaders, both our work and our character should give off the aroma of Christ.

Worldly leadership implies mastery, but a Christian is called first to be a humble follower. If you are a follower of Jesus and are also called to lead, you must live with this paradox of humility and strength.

LUKE'S SKEPTICISM OF WORLDLY LEADERSHIP

In the early chapters of the narrative, Luke's Gospel expresses a distinct skepticism about leadership. Luke critiques worldly leadership as he paints a picture of power in first-century Palestine. He grips the reader with contrasts: Those who lead in the kingdom of God are different from those in the world.

At the beginning of chapter 3, Luke uses a lot of parchment on the names of leaders: "In the fifteenth year of the reign of Tiberius Caesar—when Pontius Pilate was governor of Judea, Herod tetrarch of Galilee, his brother Philip tetrarch of Iturea and Traconitis, and Lysanias tetrarch of Abilene—during the high-priesthood of Annas and Caiaphas, the word of God came to John" (Luke 3:1-2). At the beginning of chapter 2, Luke also mentions Caesar Augustus. Why name two Caesars and the rest of these political figures? It does set the historical and geopolitical context, and it gives credibility to Luke's account, but I believe there is something more.

Luke references these leaders in sharp contrast to the heroes of his story. We recognize Tiberias's name, but the Roman Empire has fallen by the time of our reading. Herod and Pilate we recognize, but only in the context of the history-shaping life of Jesus. Despite the historical context, the likes of Caesar, Herod, Pilate, Annas, and Caiaphas are not central actors in the story being told. Rather, they are part of the landscape into which the Word of the Lord and the Holy Spirit take dramatic action.

Among human characters early in Luke's account, the most focal and significant is a vulnerable teenage girl named Mary, who welcomes the presence and movement of the Holy Spirit. The Gospel also illuminates surprising turns of provision and circumstance for the humble and faithful Zechariah and Elizabeth. John the Baptist is portrayed not as an excellent strategist but as a peculiar prophet to whom the word of the Lord arrives. These everyday characters (and not the politicians) are leaders of truly historic significance.

Leadership as the world defines it is clearly not center stage in Luke's narrative. Rather than leaders like Caesar making things happen, God is working in history, bringing surprises by the power of the Spirit despite the evil decisions of those seen as leaders. The Gospel critiques traditional power from the very beginning, casting King Herod in dark shadows of moral compromise and abuse of power. The early chapters of Luke reveal God as one who overturns established assumptions about leadership.

LUKE'S LEADERSHIP VISION

Luke contrasts the Herods, Ceasars, and Pilates of the world with a positive vision for leadership. Filled with the Holy Spirit, young Mary says of the Lord:

He has performed mighty deeds with his arm;
    he has scattered those who are proud in their
        inmost thoughts.
He has brought down rulers from their thrones
    but has lifted up the humble.
He has filled the hungry with good things
    but has sent the rich away empty. (Luke 1:51-53)

Luke's vision is of an upside-down kingdom where God is at work. His kind of leaders don't conform to the world's expectations. Rather, they carry the humility and integrity of Mary, Elizabeth, Zechariah, and John, and they cooperate with the Spirit's work in the world.

When we cooperate with the Spirit, leadership is our action in the world that intentionally creates culture and influences people.

In Genesis, God gives humankind a cultural mandate to fill the earth, subdue it, give names, and tend his creation. Our actions in the world (to create, give meaning, influence others, and shape our environment) fulfill God's mandate and create culture. Andy Crouch's thinking about culture making as leadership has expanded my vision to a holistic one that includes the artistic and prophetic as leadership.

Our intentional action toward influence and culture creation is always leadership.

This kind of leadership is not only the realm of executives and coaches. The stay-at-home parent of young children is practicing an incredibly influential form of leadership. The student and the entry-level employee practice leadership from their own social location by stewarding integrity and growth, and they influence the people and culture around them. Like Mary and Elizabeth, in God's economy those with low social position are often entrusted with leadership of special importance.

Some would say that in order to be a leader, one simply must have followers. This is true in a very basic sense—leaders lead followers and followers follow a leader. However, this perspective overlooks those who intentionally pursue a vision in faith. This intentional influence sometimes precedes the presence of followers. Like an artist whose work is appreciated only posthumously, these leaders pursue a vision and ultimately have an impact. It is not always the most obvious leaders who are changing the world! Mary, the mother of Jesus, responded faithfully to the initiative of God. She had no followers initially, but has become one of the most influential leaders in history.

From any position, the stewardship of our influence is a sacred trust from God, and it requires intentionality. As leaders, we do what we do on purpose. In this sense every Christian is called to be a leader.

Luke shows us that God himself is the protagonist of history.

Even though we create culture and influence others, we are not the center of the story. God intervenes among people. He brings down rulers from their thrones and exalts the humble, as stated in Mary's prayer (Luke 1:52). God remembers his promises and moves history toward fulfillment, as shown in Zechariah's prophecy in Luke 1:68-79.

Human beings are strong secondary characters or "supporting roles" in the drama of God, and they embrace those roles with humility and faith. As secondary characters, we cooperate with God's work in the world by following the lead of the Spirit. This cooperation requires a combination of tender humility and bold faith.

TENDER HUMILITY

As we begin to believe God's primacy in history, our frame of reference changes and as leaders we see ourselves from a humble perspective. The change of perspective is like that of Copernicus, who helped us see earth from the perspective of the sun rather than the other way around. Copernicus's insight changed astronomy, allowing us to understand orbits and their implications. It also changed how humans see ourselves within the context of the universe.

Looking from Luke's perspective, we see God at work. He chooses to move through certain humble people such as Zechariah, Elizabeth, Mary, and the shepherds of Luke 2. Mary's Magnificat prayer and Zechariah's prophecy help us see that God's purposes for us (in our small, humble journey) may actually connect with what he is doing in the world. Both Mary and Zechariah receive vision from God and are enfolded in what he is doing in history. Like Mary, all disciples are invited to accept and cooperate with the movement of the Holy Spirit and trust God to be faithful to his word.

Mary, Zechariah, and the shepherds have the humility to pay attention to their context. In their prophetic prayers, both Mary and Zechariah recite some of the real history of God's work among people. And Mary realistically notes her own humble circumstances. God's action in history does not erase the realities around us. In fact, his acts make our own circumstances more real because we know he works in the actual messes of history. This is good news for us as leaders. We don't have to be Beyoncé or Billy Graham to make a difference for the kingdom of God in remarkable ways.

BOLD FAITH

In the cases of Zechariah, Elizabeth, Mary, and the shepherds, God challenges them to act on risky, countercultural faith. Their leadership requires intentional action. Mary accepts her fate as a vulnerable single mother, trusting God to fulfill his promises in the midst of her obedience. Zechariah and Elizabeth receive a child in old age, naming him counterculturally and radically dedicating him to God.

The shepherds believe the angels, leaving their responsibility in the field and going to worship Jesus. Then they publicly proclaim the seemingly ridiculous good news. In each of these examples, humble people trusted God's communication and took risks to follow his direction. As they exercised faith, they cooperated with God's movement. Through obedience they were also shaped more in God's image and led to worship. I find it remarkable that Luke shows humble, joyful worship as a hallmark of each of these leaders.

A CYCLE: DISCIPLE AS LEADER AS DISCIPLE

If God is at work in history and he moves through humble people who cooperate with the Spirit's leading, then the dynamics of Christian leadership can be described by the simple diagram shown in figure 1.1.

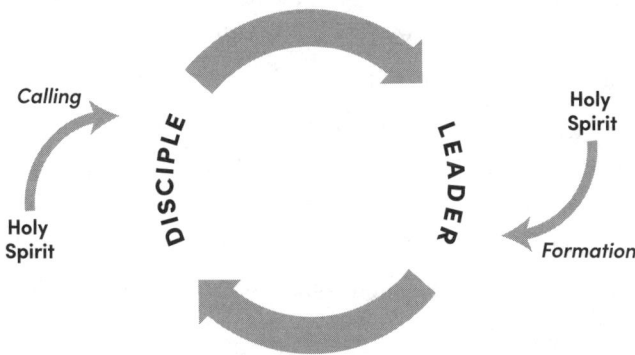

Calling

Holy
Spirit

DISCIPLE

LEADER

Holy
Spirit

Formation

Figure 1.1. The disciple/leader cycle

Leadership from a Christian perspective is a process where we continually respond to the Holy Spirit's initiative. The Spirit inspires (literally, breathes out upon) our formation as disciples who grow into the likeness of Jesus, and the Spirit also inspires vision, calling disciples into bold, vulnerable, obedient acts of leadership. Faithful leadership in turn inspires deeper formation as disciples in an ever-renewing cycle.

The formation part of the leadership diagram requires humility. We understand ourselves as apprentices of Jesus. We look to him to make us more like himself in understanding, character, relationships, integrity, and justice. As we obey the Word and the Spirit, we are shaped as disciples.

The calling part of the diagram requires faith. We must perceive and believe the invitations we receive from the Spirit, even when those invitations feel risky because they require us to believe God's direction more than our own. As we obey the Word and the Spirit, we are called and sent as leaders.

In following chapters, we will look in detail at the formation and calling process. For now, let's explore a few implications:

- *Implication 1.* Who we are and what we do must be made of the same fabric. A vision of integrity means that our spiritual formation is central to our calling and vice versa. If our discipleship must be congruent with our leadership, then we will naturally pay attention to both of them.

- *Implication 2.* If God is the protagonist of history and we are supporting characters, then we will learn to pay very close attention to what God has done in the past, what he is doing, and what's happening in his story. Like good supporting characters, we are carried by the protagonist's story as we play our humble and significant part.

- *Implication 3.* If God's work (and therefore our leadership) takes place in the context of concrete history and culture, then we will also become students of history and culture. The belief that God is involved and moving in history does not lead me to bury my head in Scripture and ignore the world around me. Rather, this frame of reference inspires me to learn from anyone and everyone! In fact, I learn a tremendous amount from secular books and courses on leadership and culture. They help me to see the landscape into which the Word of God speaks and the world the Spirit calls me into.

DISCERNMENT

In the disciple/leader cycle, we see that the Holy Spirit inspires humility as he forms us in discipleship, and the Holy Spirit inspires faith as he calls us to leadership. Navigating this path requires discernment to perceive the Spirit's leading.

In discernment, we humble ourselves before God and ask for wise direction in a particular situation. We need this wise direction in order to grow as disciples, and we also need it in order to lead faithfully. Discernment is required to receive the Holy Spirit's formation and also to receive the Holy Spirit's calling.

Where the secular leader practices strategy, the Christian leader must *first* practice discernment. Where the secular leader calculates logical risk versus reward, the Christian leader must *first* discern the invitation of the Lord and take the risk of obedience, trusting the faithfulness of God.

What does discernment look like? Discernment requires listening for the leadership of the Holy Spirit and following the direction of the Word. To listen for the Spirit, we must grow in knowledge of our own thoughts and feelings, because the Spirit leads us through our human experience. To follow the leading of God's Word, we must immerse ourselves in it, growing in love for the Word and familiarity with it over time. Discernment often requires us to pause for a while as we gain wisdom and clarity in God's timing. Finally, discernment requires us to submit ourselves to one another in Christian community.

LEADING ON THE NARROW PATH
BETWEEN FEAR AND PRIDE

As we embrace the path of tender humility and bold faith, we must also navigate the pitfalls of fear on one side and pride on the other. As

Christian leaders, we must use discernment to avoid both fear and pride. Fear is a false overfunctioning of humility that blocks obedience. Pride is a false overfunctioning of faith that takes presumptuous action rather than receiving formation as a disciple. Allow me to illustrate.

My friend Dan went through several big disruptions in his career as an analyst and leader in the energy industry. Remarkably, he ended up well after each disruption, and he even had the opportunity for an extended mission trip with his family (and mine!) between jobs. In that pause between jobs, God called Dan to start his own consulting business and provided the means to do it. Dan's gifts led the business to offer practical solutions to his customers through personal service and excellent technical insight. As with any launch of a small business, it felt like a huge risk.

On the first anniversary of the new business, we gathered as two couples for an evening of celebration to remember God's faithfulness and pray for the business into the future. It was wonderful to recount God's faithfulness over dinner. We returned to Dan's new company office to pray. He had a giant whiteboard there from the beginnings of some strategic planning. Written in large letters across the board was the word *precautionary*. It completely dominated the space.

For Susi and me, reading that word was depressing. It seemed like an invalidation of the faithfulness we had been celebrating. So we began to ask questions. By the end of the evening, we recognized together that Dan was feeling fear based on his previous career disruptions. Fear was driving him to a precautionary framework in developing the future of the work. As we prayed together, Dan recognized God's invitation to trust him more deeply. God wanted to heal the wounds of previous experiences, forming him further as a disciple. As we prayed together, the Spirit also seemed to invite Dan to trust in his own calling and the distinctive strengths of the business.

We erased the word *precautionary* and prayed for the business to be faithful in the midst of upcoming risks. In this case, Dan's "precautionary" fear was not humility at all. It was a false humility that feared he would destroy his business by making a mistake. I'm happy to say that Dan has led that business faithfully for many years since that experience. God has used his calling to shape his character as a disciple, and God has also used his leadership to serve a multitude of communities and individuals.

I had a similar experience of the Spirit's working when I faced the pitfall of pride early in my campus ministry journey. Our work at University of California at Berkeley seemed successful. The ministry had over five hundred students involved in small groups on campus, and the community was thriving. The challenge of leadership was to organize and empower enough leaders to serve the ministry well. I was supervising a staff team that, in turn, served student leaders.

I clearly remember the day I hatched a brilliant strategy to serve the ministry and enable growth. Like Moses taking Jethro's advice in Exodus 18, I decided we should appoint a new level of leaders-of-leaders among students. If we organized five smaller "congregations" serving roughly a hundred students each, we could enable care for the small group leaders and also tend to the health and growth of each congregation. It was a good idea, so I pushed it on my staff team. I limited discussion, and we selected and appointed congregation leaders.

I was very pleased—until about a month later when one of those leaders had a breakdown that caused conflict and trauma for the whole ministry. It took me over a year of pain to process the conflict of that season. On later reflection I realized my strategic move was not out of faithful discernment but out of arrogance. I was full of pride that the ministry was large and successful, and I felt I had to come up with a strategy for missional growth. When I had a good idea, I presumed that it was God's right way, but I did not listen well to the Spirit or the supervisors and team members around me. In my mind at the time, faith needed to look like further success—so I ran forward and called it faith.

I dearly wish I had paused for discernment, listened to the Spirit and the community, and gone a different way. In this case, my pride was not an abundance of faith but a lack of faith. I presumed I knew that God was leading a certain way, and I made decisions based on that assumption. I trusted myself more than I trusted God. In his grace, God used that experience to teach me a different level of humility and to lead me toward a path of true faith.

FORMED AND SENT

You, too, are called to be formed by God as a disciple and sent by God in leadership. The cycle will repeat again and again, from formation to calling and back to formation, because God is at work in history, and he uses his people as he shapes his people. In order to cooperate with the Spirit in his work to renew all of God's creation, we will need to walk a narrow path of tender humility combined with bold faith. Sometimes, like Dan, we will need to abandon fear and practice bold faith. Sometimes, like me, we will need to abandon presumptuous pride to practice tender humility. What is God's invitation to you today? In your current situation, are you tempted to fear? Are you tempted to pride? What is the Spirit saying to you as a disciple and as a leader?

This simple discipleship/leadership model gives us a distinctive shape of Christian leadership. It won't give you all the right insights for strategy, influence, and success, but it's not supposed to. It's an invitation to embark on a journey of spiritual formation integrated with your leadership. It's an invitation to engage with the deep and spiritual aspects of growing in humility and faith. I hope you also become a student of leadership science, to grow your skills in strategy and influence and creativity. There is great value in technique and effectiveness. But we must also beware of Jesus' warning later in Luke: "What good is it for someone to gain the whole world, and yet lose or forfeit their very self?" (Luke 9:25).

In the following chapters we will look closely at Luke 3 and 4 to discover the ingredients of formation and calling that will guide our development as disciples and leaders. I'm not claiming these are the only points of this section of Luke, but I think we will see their importance to leadership growth. We will observe Jesus' formation from the wilderness to the baptism, to temptation in the wilderness and into Nazareth. In each of those movements, we will find insight for our formation as leaders. I'm praying God will shape us to consistently embody leadership integrity.

PRACTICE: IMAGINATIVE PRAYER

Begin your time of prayer by settling into a relaxed position and focusing your heart and mind on God. Sometimes it helps to take a few deep breaths and consciously let go of any tensions you are holding in your body and emotions. If you are able, remember something you are grateful for and give thanks.

After you have entered into prayer, imagine yourself walking on a narrow path, with steep drops on each side. Imagine you are very motivated to reach the end of the path. Spend some time with this imaginative exercise. Engage your senses. What do you see? Hear? Smell? Feel? Taste? Note any awareness of danger on each side and the sense of care in each secure forward step.

Now consider this as a metaphor for your journey in Christian leadership. The chasm on your right is the danger of fearful self-protection. The chasm on your left is the danger of presumptuous pride. Your path forward leads to the goal where you fulfill your calling as a disciple and a leader.

Spend some time identifying how you might slip toward fear in your current situation. If you find yourself already slipping there, listen to the Holy Spirit in prayer for how you can turn from fear to courageous faith. Also spend some time identifying how you might slip toward pride. If you identify areas of prideful self-sufficiency, pray for the Spirit to soften and humble your heart.

Imagine yourself stepping forward in this season of life with a gracious combination of tender humility and bold faith. What does that combination look and feel like for you?

Spend a few minutes journaling about what you noticed in this prayer time and what help you need from God.

GROUP GUIDE 1

BIBLE STUDY: LECTIO DIVINA FOR
LUKE 1:26-56 (25 MINUTES)

This Bible study engages your group in an ancient practice called lectio divina. Latin for "divine reading," the practice is simply a way to engage a section of Scripture in contemplation. Many different guides exist for lectio divina—I'm giving you my own informal version here.

Step 1. As a group, make yourselves comfortable. Together, take a moment to read through the exercise, so you know what's coming. Consider taking a minute of silence to quiet your minds and open your hearts to God. Have one member pray a brief prayer inviting the Holy Spirit to speak to you through this text from Luke.

Step 2. Have one member of the group read the Scripture passage aloud. Listen for what stands out from the text. It could be a particular word or phrase, a feeling, a character, or an image. Take a minute of silence after the reading.

Go around your group and invite each person, if they are willing, to share just that one word or image or feeling—without any explanation.

Step 3. Have someone pray a brief prayer that God would speak further through his Word. Have a different member of the group read through the text aloud. Listen for what might be God's invitation to you through the text. Take a minute of silence after the reading.

Go around the group again, and have each person, if they are willing, share their sense of invitation from God.

Step 4. Have someone pray that God would give each person the grace to respond to his invitation. Have another member of the group read through the text aloud. As you listen, pray for God to shape your response to his invitation. Your response may be a feeling or a commitment. Don't judge what your response is, just notice it. Take a minute of silence after the reading.

Before sharing again, invite the group to commit to not judging each other's responses. As far as possible, make the group a safe space to share your authentic responses to the Word. Then go around and have each member who's willing share their response to the invitation they heard from God.

Close together in prayer.

GROUP DISCUSSION QUESTIONS FOR INTRODUCTION AND CHAPTER 1 (35 MINUTES)

Introduction

1. What is your interest in leadership? Where do you find yourself on the spectrum between reluctant leader on one side to enthusiastic leader on the other?

2. How do you think spiritual formation and leadership are related?

3. What do you most want to learn or receive from this book?

Chapter One

4. What is your response to the author's skepticism about leadership? To what extent do you share the skeptical viewpoint, and why?

5. What would it look like for your group—as individuals, but also as a community or team—to adopt a model of leadership where you follow the Spirit's lead to grow as disciples with tender humility and leaders with bold faith? (Refer to the diagram in the middle of the chapter.)

6. What would need to change?

7. How might you address the pitfalls of fear and pride?

8. What might be costs and benefits of going that way?

9. What inspires you when you consider Mary as a model of leadership?

ENCOUNTER

The Word Arrives in
the Wilderness

Lord, I pray that this chapter might illuminate ways you reveal yourself in the wilderness, raising leaders' hopes for your movement in difficult places. Holy Spirit, open leaders' hearts especially in places of desolate experiences, that they might perceive your voice. And Father, please invite some leaders into the cultivated wilderness of consecration to listen closely for your word.

At thirteen years old I had built my teen identity around athletic performance. My confidence was rooted in athletic success and the recognition that came with it. Then I experienced debilitating knee injuries lasting nearly three years and requiring multiple rounds of surgery. My confidence was shaken. I was heartbroken and, though I did not understand it at the time, I experienced a crisis of identity and vocation. In the depth of my depression, I did not know what to do or who to be. My world became a wilderness.

How often do we look for God in our dreams of success, vindication, or dominance? Do we look for him in power and control? In security or comfort? In confidence and answers? In policies and positions? Leaders are especially drawn to look in these directions. We like moving forward, looking for redemption and progress. And yet . . .

perhaps God is more likely to reveal himself in the wilderness of our experience than the promised land of our wishes. Perhaps we will find him more in questions than answers, more in challenge than comfort, more in longing than victory, more in arduous travel than in arrival at our destination. The truth is, God meets us more in our humility and weakness than in our pride and strength.

Paradoxically, formation is abundant and rich in the wilderness but often dry and scarce in the oasis. But in order to receive the formation God offers us in the wilderness, we need to first believe he will arrive there, and then learn to pay attention in specific ways.

WILDERNESS IN SCRIPTURE

Luke 3 begins with the word of God arriving to John the Baptist in the wilderness. We know from Luke 1 that John was a special, remarkable child with a miraculous birth story. And from Luke 1:80 we know he lived in the wilderness for the first thirty years of his life. In Luke 3:2 we find that the word of the Lord came to him in a particular year. It seems that John had to wait for all of those thirty years before the word came and his preaching began. John's waiting reflects the extended longing of the people of Israel after the final prophet of the Old Testament, Malachi. Four hundred years later, the word comes again to a prophet, and the crowd vibrates with expectancy.

The God of the Bible has a habit of showing up in the wilderness. Of course, he begins by walking with the man and woman in a garden, in the cool of the early evening under the trees. And occasionally he shows up in a city or a temple. But ever since men and women were banished from Eden, the Lord has visited his people in the wilderness.

Abraham entertains the threefold visitor in Genesis 18 while he sojourns in a tent along the road in a place called Mamre. "The God who sees" reassures Hagar in Genesis 21 as she shelters from the sun in the desert. Jacob wrestles with the angel of the Lord in Genesis 32 in a place where his only pillow is a rock. Moses meets the Lord, but not in the palace of Pharaoh where he grew up. After forty years of shepherding in the barren land of Midian, Moses turns aside to look, and the Lord appears in a burning desert bush in Exodus 3. The exodus story forms a strong metanarrative for the people of God, who are delivered from slavery by God's mighty hand and then sojourn in the wilderness for forty years, awaiting the fulfillment of his promise of "a land flowing with milk and honey."

Both Old and New Testaments reflect on that wilderness journey as an ongoing metaphor for the sojourning people of God, liberated but also awaiting full deliverance. We came from a garden, and we are destined for the new Jerusalem, but in the meantime we walk with God in the desert as the liminal space between the home we have left and the one God is preparing for us.

Most notably, God's true revelation in history happens in the context of a wilderness that is political, social, and also natural. God anoints Jesus the Messiah out in the country, at the Jordan River, amid social, political, and religious controversy. In Luke's narrative, the wilderness is almost a character. John, the miracle baby with dramatic destiny, grows up in the wilderness and receives the word of the Lord there. Multitudes come out to be baptized by him in the Jordan, as if they are crossing along with Joshua from the exile of wilderness into the Promised Land. The heavens are torn open as Isaiah 64 anticipates, and the Spirit descends on Jesus at his baptism. The Messiah is thus revealed not in Jerusalem but at the Jordan, in the wilderness. After Jesus' baptism the Spirit drives him again out to the desert to be tested as the people of God are tested between Egypt and Canaan.

The wilderness in Scripture is the place of testing, the place of longing and waiting, the place of suffering and survival. It is a place of isolation, a "lonely place," as Luke calls it later (5:16). The wilderness is the setting for the journey, but it is not the destination. Often it is a "trackless waste" (Psalm 107:40; Job 12:24) where we can find no path of direction or escape. We need divine help in order to be sustained in the wilderness and to be led out of it.

Yet the God of the Bible consistently reveals himself in the wilderness.

THE WILDERNESS OF EXPERIENCE

During my season of depression as an early teen, my older brother Dan experienced a deep Christian renewal. As a university student, he encountered a bright and vibrant call to give his life away in forming others as disciples of Jesus. He brought that new life to his injured punk brother—and I was dazzled by the beauty and significance and reality of the way of Jesus.

The interruption of my life and the pain of my injuries were transformed by new vision. God met me in the midst of my desolation—not in spite of it or around it. In Jesus' call I found a path of leadership I could embrace with my whole heart. In Jesus I also found the first hints that there might be meaning and power in my pain.

Several years later I was reflecting on my life in preparation for a speech at my high school graduation. I remember the sense of shock when I realized I was grateful for those injuries, because God called me and completely reoriented my life in the wilderness of my teenage depression.

This formative movement from wilderness to renewal is not a one-time experience. Rather, God often speaks to us most powerfully when we feel the weakest. In my early forties I was granted a six-month sabbatical from my InterVarsity work as a regional director. For the previous seven years I had led InterVarsity's campus work in Northern California, Hawaii, and northern Nevada. I loved the staff and the work with my whole heart, and for those years I worked harder than I had ever worked. The region was in a healthy and growing state, and I knew I needed rest and perspective. I did not yet know the extent of healing I needed. I thought I just felt tired from the work.

Only when I slowed down did I discover that I was in a wilderness period. We moved our family to Oaxaca City in southern Mexico so that I could soak in Latin American spirituality while studying integral mission models and learning from a local mentor. In many ways it was a joyful sabbatical, and I'd jump at the chance to do it again. Our family experience was both challenging (with kids in fifth and seventh grade experiencing school in a new language) and also delightful.

As soon as we arrived, however, I began having disturbing dreams every night. These nightly dreams lasted for at least four of the six months. The pattern itself overwhelmed me.

In my dreams I found myself in situations and relationships from the past seven years, always in deep tension. Often in the dream I would respond to the relationship poorly—and when I awoke, I felt deep regret. I'm not usually a crier, but I often wept in my dreams, and sometimes wept as I processed them. Thankfully, because I was on sabbatical, I had time to process my dreams every day with prayer and journaling, and I also had time to make up lost sleep.

Eventually I realized a pattern in the dreams, and I began to sense the Spirit's leadership. Each of the dreams was revealing ways the pressures of leadership had deformed my soul. Sometimes the pressures caused me to react outwardly in a way I regretted. Other times the situation made me put on a mask and outwardly perform while in my heart I reacted poorly. I began to ask God to mend my heart and lead me forward. I offered to let go of my regional director role if that would allow me to have greater integrity. I asked God what he wanted from me, and through prayer, Scripture, and my spiritual director, God asked me back, "What do *you* really want?" That question was the Spirit coming to me in the wilderness of my experience. Throughout the next few months of prayer, I experienced a renewed sense of calling that included moving into a new role.

Most simply, I came to the conviction that whatever I did in the following years, my deepest desire was to love God more and receive more of his love. It sounds simple, but this conviction brought deep healing and a new sense of freedom to me. I thank the Lord for the ways he met me in the internal wilderness of my dreams and delivered me from toxic wounds and patterns I had not previously seen.

These experiences were not my preferred path. Given the choice, I would have met God in other circumstances, not in the injury, depression, and dreams that exposed my twisted soul. I would have chosen more of a journey of strength and victory.

And yet on reflection, the painful experiences better align with my Christian theology. God is a generous Creator who empowered human beings with a cultural mandate to steward the earth and its inhabitants, reflecting his character by creating and influencing. We humans rebelled and broke fellowship with God, also damaging our relationship with each other and all creation. Now in the in-between wilderness, sojourning toward the redemptive re-creation of all things, our stewardship and creative action is intermingled with repentance and healing. By grace through the incarnation and the cross, we are rescued from slavery and invited to join the redemptive process around us while we are being redeemed. So God reveals himself in our weakness and pain, and through that revelation draws us to reveal him to the world.

ATTENTIVENESS IN THE CULTIVATED WILDERNESS OF CONSECRATION

Isaiah offers an invitation:

> See, I am doing a new thing!
>> Now it springs up; do you not perceive it?
> I am making a way in the wilderness
>> and streams in the wasteland. (Isaiah 43:19)

Often my answer to Isaiah's question, "Do you not perceive it?" is "No, I don't." In order to perceive the Spirit of God in the wilderness of our experience, we must pay attention in a certain way. I like to call it consecration: setting ourselves apart for God, ready to hear his surprising word, ready to witness his work. Consecration is a way we can practice recognizing and receiving the presence of God in difficult places. Disciplines like fasting, prayer, solitude, and silence are examples of consecration, where we intentionally hone our abilities to pay attention to the movement of God's Spirit while we quiet the other appetites that might distract us.

Our scene in Luke 3 on the banks of the Jordan River recalls another consecration, recorded in Joshua 3, where the people who have wandered in the wilderness for forty years are asked to set themselves apart. It happens at the same location—on the banks of the Jordan. After consecrating themselves, they are commanded to pay close attention to what God has done. The crossing of the Jordan is enacted as a clear echo of God's deliverance of his people at the Red Sea and also a reference to God's deliverance of his people in the first Passover. Church liturgies for baptism remember the scene in Joshua, the crossing of the Red Sea, the baptism of Jesus, and our own baptism. We find ourselves in the very same narrative.

At the Jordan of our own baptism (and every time we remember our baptism or celebrate one), we are called to set aside time and space, remember how God has moved in the past, look for his current movement, and trust in his deliverance.

God invites us to pay particular attention in situations of weakness or pain.

The long history of Christian contemplative traditions, especially that of the desert mothers and fathers, invites us to intentionally practice solitude, silence, and prayer as exercises of listening for the Word and looking for the Spirit in an internal wilderness or desert. Henri Nouwen summarizes this vision of contemplative consecration well in *The Way of the Heart*. He envisions that all our words can flow from an abundance of silence, all our relationships can flow from an abundance of solitude, and all our actions can flow from an abundance of prayer. As a leader, wouldn't you like your words, relationships, and actions to emerge from this kind of depth? Do you know anyone who seems to draw from a deep well of wisdom and maturity?

Unfortunately, I find that leaders are especially bad at the practice of contemplative consecration. We presume that we must make things happen, so we busy ourselves with action. Then when wilderness experiences come, we often feel threatened, embarrassed, or ashamed because we expect ourselves to perform well all the time. Our sense of responsibility accelerates under stress and we begin to overassociate the state of our soul with the state of our work.

Our activistic and self-protective instincts, in fact, present grave dangers to our souls in wilderness times. Idolatries and compulsions become easy drugs to ease our pain. Idolatry emerged for the Israelites in the wilderness, when they felt pressure and fear. Like narcotics, these idolatries and compulsions lead to addictions, and they snowball into toxic situations where leaders become distant, abusive, ashamed, or divided in character.

We as Christian leaders need to learn to stop, be still, and listen—especially in times of desolation. Carlo Carretto says, "God's call is mysterious; it comes in the darkness of faith. It is so fine, so subtle, that it is only with the deepest silence within us that we can hear it." I am grateful that in my own life I was given opportunities to stop and reflect. When I finally reflected on my teen experience while preparing a speech, God revealed the treasure of redemption that was hidden in my pain. In a sabbatical, God made space where I could listen to my disturbing dreams and find his deeper invitation for the next phase of my life.

I try to build regular rhythms of stopping and listening into my life. I find that when I build the rhythms into my schedule, I sometimes need to adjust them. But if I don't build them in, I never experience them. I also find that what brain scientists and innovation researchers say is true: rhythms of rest, movement, and listening help us to produce better insights, more original ideas, and deeper reflections. I believe this is true because the Holy Spirit usually moves in the wilderness. Here are a few of the rhythms that cultivate a wilderness of solitude and listening in my busy life:

- Daily: I take about fifteen minutes at the end of the day to notice where God has been present and moving in my life, and I say thank you. In the mornings, I take at least thirty minutes to reflect on Scripture and pray.

- Weekly: I take a twenty-four-hour *sabbath* where I choose not to work, and I also try to practice activities that will rest and renew my soul.

- Monthly: I take one day a month for a full-day prayer retreat. Sometimes it is focused on Bible study, other times on prayer or reflection. At least every other month I meet with a spiritual director.

- Quarterly: I try to take a longer silent retreat about three times a year where I'm away for two nights. This helps me catch up on rest enough to find a deeper state of quiet in my heart and mind.

- Annually: With my ministry team I take a weeklong Ignatian prayer retreat each year. The retreat takes place in silence but includes a conversation with a spiritual director once a day. Each time I experience this retreat I find God speaking into deep areas of my life and history that need healing and transformation.

- Every seven to ten years: I have had the privilege of a sabbatical lasting multiple months. These have always been times where God renews my calling and shapes my future.

Please don't be intimidated by the long list of practices here. I find I need them all, perhaps because I am such an action and control addict—or perhaps because I'm so deeply in need of God's care and healing. Consider for yourself, though: what one rhythm of consecration would best help you encounter God in the wilderness of your experience? Consider the concrete option described in the practice that closes this chapter.

PRACTICE: THREE-HOUR RETREAT OF SILENCE

Find a day where you can reserve three hours for silent prayer, rest, and contemplation. If possible, arrange a place where you can be relaxed and uninterrupted. I'm offering prompts and time frames below as a guide, but feel free to adapt them as needed. If you need rest, then take a brief nap. If the Spirit leads you to a different passage or reflection, follow the Spirit's lead.

PREPARATION (30 MINUTES)

When you arrive at the time and place, start by slowing down and noticing. Take note of the feelings in your body, as well as your emotions and thoughts. Consider writing those down in a journal. Sometimes writing things out helps us let go of distractions and begin to focus. Intentionally offer everything you have noticed to God. It may help to spend a few minutes breathing deeply and praying in rhythm with your breath:

Inhale: "Lord, I'm here."
Exhale: "Lord, I offer myself to you."
Inhale: "Lord, I'm here."
Exhale: "Lord, please speak to me."
(Repeat.)

REMEMBRANCE (5-15 MINUTES)

Spend a short time remembering a time when you felt close to God or had real joy. Savor that memory. Write down as many of the details as you can. Give thanks to God, and continue remembering.

SCRIPTURE (30-60 MINUTES)

When you feel that you're ready, read Isaiah 40:1-5 slowly a few times. Note what stands out to you and what makes you curious. With the passage from Isaiah in mind, consider journaling about one or more of the following prompts:

- Reflect on a challenging "wilderness" time in your life. What made it challenging? Tell God what the experience was like and ask him to speak tenderly to you about it. Wait and see if you sense God speaking to you in response.

- Ask the Lord how he wants to use that wilderness experience to "prepare the way" for you to meet him. God does not intend pain for his people, but he sometimes uses difficult experiences redemptively to meet us. Wait and see how God may respond.

- Ask the Lord how he may want to reveal his glory, as in verse 5. Listen and notice how he might respond.

RELAXATION (30-60 MINUTES)

Go for a walk if you're able, or just observe the setting around you. Ask God to speak to you as you relax and move or observe. Don't force yourself by trying to be profound—just open yourself to God and notice what beauty or truth he may want to reveal to you. As you relax your mind, you may notice God speaking to you out of your reflections on the Isaiah passage or in other ways. Just take note of what you sense and thank God for it. You may also notice tensions or anxieties coming up. If so, just gently hold those before God and ask God to speak comfort to you.

CONCLUSION (15-30 MINUTES)

When you return to your place, read over Isaiah 40:1-5 once more and write down what you are hearing from God. Ask him for what you need in order to be faithful to him. Give thanks and ask if he has anything else to say to you. Take note of what you may hear.

CONTEXT MATTERS

The Spirit Prepares the Way

Lord, open our eyes to the wilderness of our context. Give us capacity to perceive the topography of resources, relationships, and power both in ourselves and around us. Grant us the eyes of the Father who "looks kindly on the lowly" (Psalm 138:6). And Lord, we boldly ask that you would help us see ourselves more clearly in the complexity of our social location. Make us leaders who see ourselves and others well and can therefore love with wise discernment. Please, Lord Jesus, proclaim your good news in the wilderness where we live and lead.

In college I learned to lead Bible studies. First I learned by participating. Then I was an apprentice, and eventually I led my own groups and trained apprentices myself. The studies were absolutely transformational. I had progressed in my mind from Paduan to Jedi Master, especially in the Gospel of Mark. So when I moved across the San Francisco Bay from Stanford to Berkeley to join InterVarsity staff, I jumped right in leading first-year students through a study of Mark.

A few weeks in I was puzzled. Students were not responding in the ways I had expected or hoped. The group had not gained the cohesion and momentum I wanted. Something about my Jedi Bible study skills seemed to be backfiring. When I talked this over with my supervisor Dana, she helped me see how different this group and context were from what I had previously experienced.

Berkeley was different from Stanford as a city and as a campus. My group was more diverse culturally than I had experienced in the past and more different from my own cultural background. Dana then helped me to see myself differently by suggesting I ask some questions. I went individually to each member of that Bible study (around sixteen of them) and asked, "What do you experience in my leadership of our study?" and, "What would make you want to stay in this study to the end?" Then I simply listened without explaining or defending.

That experience opened a treasure trove of cultural learning for me. The conversations were challenging for me, and often more difficult for the students, because of cultural and power dynamics. Some of them didn't initially feel safe speaking honestly about my impact on them. I often needed to ask questions multiple times in order to demonstrate that I was really listening. But by God's mercy, I began to learn!

I learned that some of my supposed Jedi skills were driving students away and causing division in the group. I learned that my own impact on others was different from what I had assumed. For example, I used a direct form of group conflict communication, which worked for me but evoked shame in some Asian American students in the group. Blessed by new sight, I proceeded in some very different ways. These changes were challenging for me, almost like learning a new language. I needed help from the students, but I learned new ways to communicate and lead. By God's great mercy, the entire group recommitted to our study, and we had a wonderful time studying Mark over two years.

As leaders and disciples, we exist in a particular context. In this chapter we will explore how the Holy Spirit shapes our leadership distinctly in our contexts so we can better influence people and create culture.

JOHN'S WILDERNESS

John the Baptist's ministry takes place in a multifaceted wilderness. John's wilderness is literal, but it is also more than that. The word of the Lord compels John to preach a baptism of repentance for the forgiveness of sins. Those ideas of repentance and forgiveness invoke the inner wilderness of guilt and shame—and our hope for cleansing.

John's preaching seems to reach a huge diversity of people, from Jewish leaders to Roman soldiers to peasants and tax collectors. Those who have two coats are asked to share one with the poor (who are presumably also present and listening). The soldiers are told to turn from violence, not to lie, and to be content. The tax collectors are told to be honest and not extort. Children of Abraham are invited to be humble, fear the Lord, and consider themselves not spiritually superior, but rather in need of salvation. In his preaching John addresses dynamics of power, economics, politics, religion, and culture.

For John, "a baptism of repentance for the forgiveness of sins" (Luke 3:3) takes place in the world of religion but also in the context of social, political, and economic relationships. Luke gives us a metaphor for this: Isaiah's vision of the topography of the wilderness. Isaiah imagines a massive public works project: building a highway through mountains and valleys. The envisioned highway is the expensive kind, built for a king or emperor. The road must be smooth and straight and level. This highway, Isaiah says, is meant not just for an emperor but for God himself. To build this highway through the wilderness, the hills must be brought down, the valleys filled up, and the crooked places made straight.

The mountains, valleys, and crooked paths John preaches about are in and among the people. He speaks of generosity, saying no to violence, and reversing unjust practices. Can you see the connection? The word of the Lord comes to the wilderness and is spoken by John. That word, according to Isaiah, is meant to prepare the way for the Lord, lowering mountains and filling valleys. And when John's word of repentance comes, the mountains and valleys involve politics, religion, and economics.

Put another way, the spiritual landscape of the wilderness involves the social landscape of power. As we saw in the last chapter, the wilderness in Luke's Gospel refers to the liminal space of our suffering and waiting. But through John's preaching, we see that the wilderness is also our social context.

Imagine your family, neighborhood, organization, or professional community as a landscape. What do the hills and valleys look like? Who or what is on top in terms of power and influence, and who is in the deepest valley? What about resources? What roads provide connection, understanding, and communication? To what extent can individuals, families, or affinity groups change their location? And how would you describe the spiritual topography of your context? Who has spiritual power or influence? Where is the greatest spiritual need or pain? I find it helpful to periodically do this exercise by drawing pictures or maps to describe power, privilege, and need in my social context. I always see something new when I pause to reflect this way.

It is important when looking at our context to consider as many dimensions of diversity as possible: race, ethnicity, nationality, gender, class, political affiliation, education, wealth, and sexuality, to name a few. When we take the time to engage with varied human experiences and identities, we begin to see a complex wilderness with metaphorical mountains and valleys. The dynamics of power, resources, and culture often leave people feeling desolate or volatile. The good news is that God keeps showing up in the wilderness.

Understanding the wilderness of our context helps leaders in two ways. First, when we see the community around us, we are more able to see ourselves and grow. Second, a clear vision of our context helps us to serve with righteousness and with greater effectiveness.

Jesus' incarnation shocks us with particularity. God himself has entered history in the flesh, with specific ethnicity and culture, location and time, gender, class, and family. Whether our leadership involves transforming a small family or ruling a nation, we influence particular people in particular situations. We, too, occupy specific locations in history and society. But we are often blind to these realities. Like proverbial fish, we don't recognize the water around us.

In my Bible study at Berkeley, I made assumptions about how to communicate and form a group. They were effective strategies in my previous context! Clearly those strategies were ineffective in my new community, but they pointed to a deeper opportunity for me. Dana's excellent leadership presented me the chance to see myself more clearly and to understand others better.

As a highly educated White American male, I came into the Bible study with certain assumptions and blind spots. When I asked for feedback, I learned that my assumptions did not apply to most of the students in my group. As a result, I took on the role of learner. I learned how my assumptions could hurt the group dynamic and how to better serve those in the study. As I continued to watch and listen, I slowly grew in cultural competency. Ultimately, my learning enabled me to lead the group into the Scriptures more effectively.

At the same time I was becoming aware of my own cultural tendencies. For example, only when I recognized the value and beauty of indirect communication could I see how direct my communication was. Only when I asked members of the group, "What do you experience in my leadership?" did I discover the ways my tendencies impacted individuals and the group. As I recognized the impact, I was able to adjust my leadership.

In addition to cultural differences, I recognized the power of dominance in my leadership. Dominance itself made me blind to dominance and therefore less aware of myself. For example, in the United States, we assume that direct communication is the way to do business. Because direct cultures have long been the majority controlling government and commerce, we assume that these ways are "normal." And because they seem normal, those of us with dominant cultural tendencies often don't see others. We don't have to. So I as a White American male was able to thrive with my direct communication and did not need to recognize it as a cultural or dominant trait. I was blind to it.

In contrast, those who live in the United States with indirect communication tendencies are *very* aware of these differences. As I asked open-ended questions of my students, I learned of their culture, but I also learned of my power. Dominant-culture power is not bad in itself, but it exercises a large impact on nondominant people and groups. When I became more aware of my tendencies, I was able to meet the students in ways that honored them and their families. I didn't leave my culture behind, but once I recognized it, I was able to adjust my leadership style to fit the real people before me. When I saw the social topography around me, I was able to see myself and lead more effectively.

The experience of asking for feedback did more than improve my leadership. In John the Baptist's language, it allowed me to repent, be forgiven, and grow in intimacy with God. God's gracious and severe light revealed my cultural traits and my dominance, and it also showed how I was blindly marginalizing my students. The open-ended conversations with my students showed me ways I was lacking in love. I received forgiveness from my students and from God, and I took the opportunity to change direction. Because of forgiveness from God and others, the situation was actually liberating in the end. It freed me to learn, love, and lead in new ways.

GOD'S PREFERENTIAL OPTION

Roman Catholic teaching refers to "God's preferential option for the poor," a term coined by Jesuit priest Father Pedro Arrupe. This language points to an observation throughout Scripture: that God seems to pay especially close attention and show special love to those at the margins—not only the economically poor but also those with little power or voice.

I have often struggled with the proposal that God prefers the poor. Isn't God fair? Doesn't God love rich and poor equally? And what about those in the middle? And yet there it is all over Scripture, that God will pay special attention to those on the margins of the world. In Luke 3, John the Baptist preaches repentance to those with various kinds of power: those with wealth (or at least clothing), tax collectors, soldiers, and Jewish leaders. In each case John's command seems to prefer the poor. Why might God show special love for the poor?

There are multiple valid answers to these questions. Some reference the systemic inequities that need to be remedied for the sake of God's justice. Some claim that evil spiritual powers inhabit the structures of empire and wealth, and God naturally opposes those powers and prefers the humble poor. Others emphasize God's desire to bring shalom—a holistic spiritual, social, and economic peace and harmony— to the whole world, beginning with the lowly. Still others propose that in order to reach a whole community, God starts by transforming the most needy and then proceeds to others in a "trickle-up" dynamic. These are all worthy of further study, but for the sake of spiritual formation and leadership, I will focus on the dynamics of grace.

God loves showing grace—literally, showing unmerited favor toward those of us who don't merit favor. In fact, grace is one of the defining elements of God's character. Throughout the story of the Old Testament God often chooses losers, outcasts, and small ones to receive his love. Think of Joseph, Benjamin, Jacob, and David. Think also of Ruth, Rahab, and Hagar. In reference to all of Israel, Deuteronomy 7:6-7 says:

> For you are a people holy to the LORD your God. The LORD your God has chosen you out of all the peoples on the face of the earth to be his people, his treasured possession.
>
> The LORD did not set his affection on you and choose you because you were more numerous than other peoples, for you were the fewest of all peoples.

Grace, by its very nature, is given in places of lack and need. It springs up in situations of humility, poverty, and powerlessness. If God loves to move with grace, what does that mean for the Christian leader?

It means leaders must look for grace to emerge especially at the margins of our social landscape. We must become attentive to the ways God loves to move. His tendency is to spring up grace in surprising scenarios. We must be open to the ways God chooses people and programs, strategies and movements. Nobody expected Zechariah, Elizabeth, Mary, Joseph, John, or Jesus to be critical characters in the redemption of the world.

This means that in order to pay attention to God's movements of grace, Christian leaders must practice a preference for the poor. It takes practice, because the world often draws our attention the opposite direction.

To be clear, I don't think this means we ignore or oppose those with privilege and power. And it does not mean justice and advocacy are the only valid forms of Christian work. Jesus himself gracefully engages those with wealth and power. However, the dynamics of grace point us to a distinctive love for those who are disempowered and a powerful curiosity about the social landscape around us. Our leadership will be more Christian (and, I believe, more effective) to the extent that we pay special attention to the poor or marginalized.

In our leadership context, we will often encounter tensions and decision points. At those points of decision, grace will ask first about the impact to those on the margins. Grace will consider that impact with greater emphasis than the impact on those with power. At points of decision, leaders tuned to grace will also ask questions to learn directly from those who are most vulnerable.

In my Bible study in Berkeley, I consulted Dana as my wise supervisor in a moment of tension and decision. She counseled me from the perspective of grace to ask open-ended questions of my students. What might this look like in your context? Who might you consult in order to best learn how to embody grace in your leadership?

I have received hospitality from Christians who are truly poor on a global scale, and in that experience I saw grace in ways I never would have otherwise. In homes and churches of poor, rural families in Mexico, I received a loving generosity flowing from encounters with Jesus. In urban squatter communities in the Philippines, I encountered joy and faith that defied my understanding. I have tasted something of God's especially generous and joyful love for the poor, and that taste inspires a growing hunger in me.

However, my calling continues to focus on the relatively privileged world of North American universities. For me, that means I regularly ask questions of those students and staff who are most vulnerable. I try to practice seeing the social topography around me, looking for grace. As I pray for my work and my community, I invite God to help me see myself and the world more clearly.

PRACTICE: GOSPEL CONTEMPLATION

Read Luke 3:1-20 once to familiarize yourself with the story. Then read again slowly and imagine the scene, trying to engage all of your senses. What does it look like where John is baptizing? What is the crowd like? How do people react when they hear John's words?

Read one more time slowly, but put John's ministry in the context of the community that surrounds you in your neighborhood or professional setting. Who comes forward to ask John, "What should we do then?" (Luke 3:10). What does John say to them? In the end, imagine yourself asking John that question. What does John say to you?

GROUP GUIDE 2

Read Luke 3:1-20. Take a few minutes to look over the passage individually, making any notes you wish.

Then as a group, consider the following questions together. Make sure to listen well to one another and build on each other's insights.

Observe

- What do you notice about the word of God?
- What do you notice about the Holy Spirit?
- What do you notice about the context of John the Baptist's ministry?

Interpret

- How might John's ministry be preparing the way as descried in Isaiah 40, as quoted in verses 4-6?
- What might be the significance of the wilderness in this section, literally and metaphorically?

Apply

- How is God preparing the way for you to encounter Jesus?
- When you ask, "What should we do then?" as in verse 10, what might John say to you?

**GROUP DISCUSSION QUESTIONS FOR
CHAPTERS 2–3 (25 MINUTES)**

1. How might your group perceive God's presence and movement in the wilderness?
2. How has God revealed himself in the wilderness of your experiences of suffering or challenge?

3. What disciplines of consecration are you trying, and how are they working for you?

4. How would you describe the landscape of your context in terms of power, resources, and social differences?

5. How do you think God sees that landscape? What might he think and feel about it?

6. What are the implications of that landscape for your leadership?

FORMATION

The Gifts of Baptism

Lord, we need to be filled at the most fundamental levels with your love and blessing. Speak to us, Father, of our identity and belovedness. Anoint us, Holy Spirit, with your power and truth. Lead us, Jesus, to become more like you. Heal and bless us in the deep places of our identity. Make us, Lord, like the tree of Psalm 1 and Jeremiah 17, planted and extending our roots to the waters of life.

The most important thing about you is not what you do, what you know, or what you feel. The most important thing about you is *who you are.*

God knows you completely and loves you. You are of inherent value aside from what you achieve or how you may fail. God created you (and all of creation) out of joyful, loving, overflowing triune community. Who you are is also fundamental to how you are called to lead.

Why is it so difficult to believe and remember these truths? The impulses within us and the messages around us tell a different story. The systems and empires of the world use humans for their own purposes. Our communities (and sometimes even our families) value us more for our contribution or production than for our inherent presence.

According to Scripture, these dynamics are the legacy of sin. Sin stains and deforms the image of God in people. The influences that call us to worship productivity, wealth, or power are so prevalent that they soak into our souls, convincing us we exist to work, produce, impress, and avoid mistakes. And then our own insecurity often reinforces the messages around us, causing us to seek love and security through shortcuts of performance, control, appearance, or addiction. Leadership involves action in the world, but it is designed to flow with integrity from our true selves.

In my early twenties I was introduced to Adult Children of Alcoholics (ACA) literature. My dad was an alcoholic, though I never experienced his drinking. He was dramatically converted to following Jesus around the time I was born, and Dad never had a drink after that time. In my twenties I was exploring my own family systems, so I picked up an ACA book. I was shocked to find my temperamental performance orientation so clearly described. A thin little book showed me how I used achievement to control the emotional systems of my family and to manage how I felt about myself. This experience made me more aware of my family pain and the ways I react to it.

We each have shortcuts to manage how we feel about ourselves, and leaders are particularly susceptible to gaining value from production or performance. In light of this, the story of Jesus' baptism is meant to shock us and reveal a different way. The baptism of Jesus points us to the most fundamental principle of Christian leadership.

RECEIVING IDENTITY, AFFECTION, AND PLEASURE FROM GOD

Let's look at Luke 3:21-37. By the middle of Luke 3, the reader anticipates that Jesus will arrive and lead with power. The word has come in the wilderness, and the Spirit has prepared the way. The ministry of John levels mountains and fills valleys: he straightens a road in the social topography of Israel to get people ready to see God's salvation together. John then predicts the power of the coming Messiah: he will baptize with the Holy Spirit and fire. He will gather the good wheat of the people and burn up the chaff. The Messiah is going to come and perform a bunch of impressive stuff!

But when Jesus does arrive, he begins by receiving.

> When all the people were being baptized, Jesus was baptized too. And as he was praying, heaven was opened and the Holy Spirit descended on him in bodily form like a dove. And a voice came from heaven: "You are my Son, whom I love; with you I am well pleased." (Luke 3:21-22)

Why does Luke introduce Jesus this way? Why might Jesus have begun his ministry leadership with baptism?

- Before Jesus the Son of God speaks of his Father, he receives affirmation of his beloved sonship.
- Before Jesus the Good Shepherd expresses love to those in his care, he listens to the Father calling him beloved.
- Before Jesus the Messiah (literally, in Greek, "the anointed one") begins to baptize others with the Holy Spirit, he experiences the Spirit anointing him in a bodily, multisensory way.
- Before Jesus our Lord and leader begins the work of redemption, he receives the Father's unqualified pleasure in him.

Many years ago, my spiritual director Father Tom introduced me to various practices from Eastern Orthodox spirituality. Those practices expanded my perspective and fed my soul. I learned to pray with icons, which are visual, theological representations of particular passages of Scripture. Icons are said to be written (not painted or drawn), to emphasize the fact that they are expressions of study and prayer and not simply artistic works. I invite you to explore the scene of Jesus' baptism in Luke 3 through reflecting on the image shown in figure 4.1. (For a color version visit https://prayericons.com/project/baptism-of -christ.) Read along below the icon for a guide to your reflections.

Figure 4.1. The baptism of Jesus

Prayerful observation of the icon is a powerful way to reflect on the biblical text in its broader theological context. An important element to recognize about icons is that they often employ inverse perspective. Rather than traditional perspective where lines of sight converge on the horizon (think of a road looking narrower into the distance), in icons the lines of sight often converge on the viewer. This is intentional—the inverse perspective brings the one viewing or praying with an icon into the story. The baptism icon here puts the viewer in the river with Jesus.

The large shape of the icon reflects its theological significance. This icon and the Luke 3 narrative accompany the Orthodox feast of the theophany—literally, the revelation of God. The baptism is one of the few places in Scripture where Father, Son, and Holy Spirit are shown together. Notice the semicircle at the top, indicating the heavens opening, and the downward motion of one ray that becomes three. The heavens that were closed by Adam's sin have been opened by Jesus' arrival. The Spirit is represented by the image of a dove. The voice of the Father is implied in the open heaven and rays toward the Son.

The water completely envelops the image of Jesus. This represents the narrative of Jesus' entire life—from his birth (always shown in icons in a cave-shaped space), to his placement in the tomb. In this way all of Jesus' redemptive work is represented in the moment of his anointing. We can be encouraged as we contemplate the way the full Trinity is engaged in the moment of Jesus' baptism. As we see the Father blessing Jesus in his life from beginning to end, we can imagine that blessing for our own lives. As the Spirit anoints Jesus' life at his baptism, we can know the Spirit's blessing of our lives from beginning to end. Jesus' birth, baptism, and death are all congruent in direction, beauty, and trinitarian agreement.

Notice also the implied movement of the image. The river Jordan flows outward to the edge of the icon, encouraging observers to see themselves in the waters of Jesus' baptism and to remember their own baptism. Jesus' posture is significant as well. He receives the image's implied motion in three ways. First, the Spirit descending and the Father speaking seem to move toward Jesus from top to bottom. Second, John's witness moves toward Jesus from the side, with an open hand that points to Jesus' head. Both of these show Jesus receiving his identity. He fully becomes the Messiah (anointed one) when the anointing of the Spirit dramatically rests on him. He does not assert his identity by proclamation, but rather allows John to proclaim him as the one who will baptize with the Spirit and with fire. Finally, Jesus' face is inclined downward to emphasize the humble outpouring trajectory of his life (in Greek, *kenosis*). This sense of downward movement of Father, Spirit, and Son expresses the unified self-giving nature and energy of the Trinity. The dynamic of God's downward motion combines with the river flowing out toward the praying observer, encouraging us to receive God's self-giving love. All these elements of posture and movement draw me to reflect on how Jesus was filled up with the same love and power he pours out on us.

The three angels on the right side of the river symbolize the sovereignty of God by expressing the participation of heaven in the earthly reality of Jesus' experience. Jesus' right hand extends in blessing toward the waters. While the baptism of John represented turning and cleansing from sin, Jesus enters the waters sinless and extends his blessing, then, toward the waters of *our* baptism. When Orthodox believers remember and celebrate the feast of the baptism of Jesus, they bless a huge vat of water, which becomes holy water for the rest of the year. This may seem strange to Protestants, but it represents the way Christian baptism is different from that of John the Baptist. Because of Jesus, our baptism is more than simply repentance for forgiveness of sins (though it is also that). Christian baptism also unites us with Jesus, making us part of his body. The waters of baptism are blessing, not just cleansing! Christ in his humble nakedness is the new Adam, able to wash us from past stains but also able to clothe us with his own righteousness. As the icon shows Jesus blessing the waters and making them holy, so also he blesses his people with his holiness.

You might notice fish and some small characters below Jesus in the water. These help us see the baptism in broader biblical context. The man in the waters on the lower left traditionally represents a personification of the Jordan River, while the woman on the right represents the Red Sea. Jesus' body divides the water. Just as God delivered Israel from slavery across the sea and brought his people into the Promised Land across the river, so Jesus delivers his people out of slavery and into promise through baptism. As we are delivered, we become the very container of his presence in the world, as described in Psalm 114:1-3:

> When Israel came out of Egypt,
>   Jacob from a people of foreign tongue,
> Judah became God's sanctuary,
>   Israel his dominion.

The sea looked and fled,
  the Jordan turned back.

The sea creature on the bottom right of the image represents powers of chaos in the waters, as referenced in Psalm 74:13-14:

It was you who split open the sea by your power;
  you broke the heads of the monster in the waters.
It was you who crushed the heads of Leviathan
  and gave it as food to the creatures of the desert.

In the Orthodox liturgies of the baptism of Jesus, we also remember the drama of Elijah and Elisha crossing the Jordan River in 2 Kings 2:6-14. One of the prayers from the liturgy reads, "The river Jordan once turned back before the mantle of Elisha, after Elijah had been taken up into heaven, and the waters were divided on this side and on that: the stream became a dry path before him, forming a true figure of the baptism whereby we pass over the changeful course of life. Christ has appeared in the Jordan to sanctify the waters." As I pray with Jesus' baptism, I also find myself in the story of God's people, miraculously delivered by his power.

BAPTISM AND LEADERSHIP FORMATION

As Stephen Covey has famously said, "The main thing is to keep the main thing the main thing." For disciples who are leaders who are disciples, we must begin like Jesus: with the identity, affection, and pleasure God gives us. We are not the protagonists of the story, and we don't lead from our own strength. Identity, affection, and pleasure are the "main thing" of our growth, both as disciples and leaders. The baptism of Jesus gives us an amazing combination of perspectives. We find God's triune identity demonstrated in the narrative and shape of the scene, and at the same time we are invited to consider our own identity in light of our baptism. God's identity and affection are demonstrated and offered to us. We remember that God is the one who names, affirms, anoints, and calls us before we do anything. I personally find that when I'm struggling as a disciple or leader, the affirmations of the baptism get to the root of my issues.

Identity: "You are my son or daughter." My identity is not in my success or failure. It is not in my history or brokenness. My identity is not in my job, my skills, or special characteristics. Rather, I am chosen and known by the God who created me. When I know my identity, I become able to discern God's calling.

Affection: "You are the beloved." God sees me and loves me. He really sees me and actually loves me. Really. God's love is able, over time, to dissolve my insecurity and heal my wounds. Our deepest wounds and most persistent compulsions usually come from loss or failure of love. Filled with the love of God, I no longer need to live for the affection or approval of others. The immense volume and mass of his love are able to fill every need in me and around me. When God soaks me in his love, I become more absorbent. Somehow the fibers of my soul become full of love, and I'm more at peace. I'm more able to love others. I gain secure humility. I'm more able to trust him with my formation and calling.

Pleasure: "I am well pleased with you." The pleasure of God rests on our identity and God's affection and not on our performance. Like Jesus, we receive his pleasure before we do anything. Our growth as disciples and our work as leaders take on a distinct character when they flow out of the pleasure God already has in us (rather than flowing from insecurity, trying to gain his approval or pleasure). Repentance, obedience, and faithful leadership taste best when they are compelled by God's joy. I can't overstate the importance of this: God's pleasure precedes our productivity. When we look for joy primarily in the results of our work, we get the order wrong—good work flows from God's joy.

The identity, affection, and pleasure we receive from God are the "main thing" I come back to again and again as a disciple and a leader.

WHY THE GENEALOGY?

Why in the world does Luke follow the baptism of Jesus with his genealogy? From my American sensibilities, it seems ridiculous to include
the long list of names between Jesus' baptism and his temptation in
the wilderness.

And yet our human families, communities, and identities are the
most formative and deformative forces in our lives. Though the genealogy contains some significant Easter eggs (for example, Jesus'
priestly heritage and royal connection to David), I think it stands
mainly as a reminder that our calling as disciples and leaders is always
steeped in family and cultural heritage. The foundational identity, affection, and pleasure of God speak to us as embodied, encultured
people who always have family issues. We come to our baptism, and
to our calling as disciples and leaders, with the texture of our distinct
history and heritage.

My wife and I recently attended a neighborhood party. The hosts
are delightful people and amazing neighbors. While sitting on the
screened porch and chatting with these neighbors' adult daughter, another neighbor referred to our host, saying, "You've got the best dad."
With wisdom beyond her age, the young woman responded with
something like, "He's great, but every family has its issues and every
kid has a rough experience." Indeed, every family has issues—even the
ones that seem healthy

Luke's inclusion of the genealogy encourages me to continue engaging psychological therapy as part of my growth as a disciple and
leader. In my midtwenties I experienced some confusing dynamics in
the team I was leading. When I reflected on the dynamics and asked
a mentor about them, I began to recognize that my family of origin
issues *might* be related, so I entered therapy. Of course in therapy, I
looked closely at my family issues, including having an alcoholic
parent. In short order I discovered that my issues were choreographing
the whole unhealthy dance of the team! Once I saw this, I was able to
begin changing and growing. I thank God for that chance to learn

about my own brokenness and sin in the context of my imperfect family. Like any family, mine has been a powerful source of love and blessing, as well as a source of pain and loss. Therapy has helped me in multiple seasons of life. Our family and cultural issues are often difficult to see without skilled help. When we do see them, we are able to receive the identity, affection, and pleasure of God in deeper ways.

I encourage all disciples and leaders: go to therapy when the opportunity is ripe. When you begin to see the shape of some of your issues and struggles, go to therapy. When you have insurance that will help you pay, go to therapy! Why this blanket encouragement? The baptism and the genealogy are related. As disciples, we are all limited in our formation to the extent that we are blind to our issues. And as leaders, we will always transmit our unknown and unhealed issues into the culture we create.

The genealogy also helps validate the place of cultural identity in our growth as disciples and leaders. Jesus came not just from a family line, but a cultural story. He bore identities such as Israelite, religious Jew, member of an oppressed people under empire, male, refugee, working class, Nazarene. Each identity was associated with a narrative and a set of experiences. The genealogy points to those narratives and experiences by tracing history.

Into these experiences the Father spoke identity to Jesus by naming him beloved Son. As beloved Son, he was no less Israelite, or oppressed, or working class—the story of his life to that point was the same—but he was called to something deeper. We all similarly carry many valid identities. In each area where our experience or history connects us to community and story, we inhabit an aspect of identity.

The most important thing about you is not what you do, but who you are. Luke emphasizes this reality by revealing the scene of Jesus' baptism and adding his genealogy—right at the beginning of his ministry and before he accomplishes anything. This scene is an invitation to you. Consider your own baptism in light of Jesus' baptism. How does the Father speak identity, affection, and pleasure into your life, and what difference does that make for you? What do you notice of the Holy Spirit's work in your life? And how might you follow Jesus in the radical act of surrender to God's love and leadership? Considering the genealogy, what aspects of identity and heritage do you carry from your history and experiences? How does the baptism inform or transform those?

PRACTICE: PRAY WITH THE BAPTISM ICON

I invite you to take fifteen to thirty minutes in quiet. Situate yourself with the baptism icon discussed in this chapter in view. If you prefer, you can find a high-resolution color version of the icon at https://prayericons.com/project/baptism-of-christ.

Read through Luke 3:21-22 slowly twice and imagine the scene. Then patiently look at the icon. Ask God to draw your attention to the elements he wants you to pray about. Notice how your thoughts and feelings are moved as you look at the image and imagine the scene. When you have a sense of focus on a particular element, stay there. The prompts below relate to specific elements I describe about the icon. If any of those elements draw you, feel free to follow the prompts in your prayers.

Imagine the story of Jesus' baptism. Consider the profound blessing he receives from the words of the Father and the descent of the Spirit. Ask God to speak his words of anointing and blessing on your life, then be quiet and listen. If you sense something from the Spirit, ask for more—more clarification or meaning or detail. Consider asking the Spirit for his words of blessing for each specific phase of your life.

Reflect on the movement of the baptism icon. Find yourself in the flow of the river of Jesus' baptism. Imagine the downward and outward flow of blessing and anointing. Give thanks to Jesus for descending, humbling himself, and pouring himself out for you.

Spend time with the theme of blessing. Considering the angels on the right side of the image, ask God to show you the participation of heaven in the movements of your life. How has God been present in your story, even when you might not have noticed it? Imagine the waters being cleansed by Jesus' baptism and turned into a blessing of holiness and joy on your life. Ask Jesus to make your own baptism real to your experience today.

Consider deliverance themes. In the story of your life, what has God saved or delivered you from? Ask the Holy Spirit to show you more about your own deliverance. Wait and listen.

GROUP GUIDE 3

BIBLE STUDY: LUKE 3:21-38 (25 MINUTES)

Start by reading Luke 3:21-22.

- Imagine the scene and describe as much as you can together. How do you think it looked, sounded, felt, and smelled from Jesus' perspective? From John's perspective? From the crowd's perspective?
- If *you* experienced what Jesus experienced in this passage, what would the significance be for you? What difference might it make?

Continue with the genealogy, Luke 3:23-38. Read it aloud.

- What did you notice, and what significance might it have?
- Note any names you recognized. What might their significance be?
- Consider the baptism and the genealogy together. What might the two of them represent together that neither would on its own?

For application:

- Reflect on your sense of calling as a leader. What might the baptism of Jesus mean practically for your leadership in the next week?

GROUP DISCUSSION QUESTIONS FOR CHAPTER 4 (35 MINUTES)

1. What differences and similarities did you note between studying the passage in traditional Bible study and contemplating the baptism icon?

2. How has God spoken identity, affection, and pleasure into your life? How have other people communicated those things to you? What difference does it make for you day to day?

3. Where might you want or need God to confer identity, affection, or pleasure to you?

4. What might it look like for your group or team to be healed, formed, and secure in God at the deepest level?

5

RADICAL REST

Sabbath Keeping

Lord, as leaders we need your mercy and care in particular ways. Teach us "the unforced rhythms of grace" (Matthew 11:28-30, MSG) that lead us from rest to work and back to rest.

Scottish athlete and missionary Eric Liddell, whose story is told in the movie *Chariots of Fire*, was a favorite to win the hundred-meter sprint in the 1924 Paris Olympics. When he learned that the final would be run on a Sunday, he refused to run due to his Christian convictions about the sabbath. Liddell was considered a fool by many and criticized heavily by the media, but he stuck to his convictions and did not race. In a dramatic turnaround, Liddell then raced the four hundred meter (for which he did not train) and decisively won the Olympic gold. In the end, Liddell's enduring legacy is not his unlikely gold medal. He is famous for what he did not do. It can be true for us as well: what we don't do can be as significant to our leadership as what we do.

From the very beginning, a radical pattern was built into creation. The word *radical* in its most literal form means "from the root." The core of the word is from the Latin *radix*. The word has come to mean "extreme" or "revolutionary," but it got there through subterranean paths. You see, characters or causes arrive at full commitment only if their commitment goes to the deepest level, the level of the root. The pattern of sabbath keeping is radical in both senses: it is foundational, at the roots of creation—and it is also revolutionary. Rhythms of rest can be an antidote to many of the forces of cultural and family brokenness that impede our formation. These rhythms can bring us back to the baptism of Jesus and the identity, affection, and pleasure that shape our souls at the deepest level. This is particularly crucial for leaders who are tempted to the idolatry of work.

When the Lord commands sabbath keeping in Exodus 20, he refers all the way back to the beginning. When God created everything and saw that it was good, he then rested on the seventh day. And so the Lord commands that his people set apart one day per week, devoting it completely to God in rest and worship. In this way, the pattern of sabbath keeping extends back to our historic roots and goes as deep as our created identity.

Sabbath keeping is revolutionary in the sense that it actively resists the forces of idolatry and empire. Where the systems of our world promote productivity and profit, sabbath invites us regularly to *stop* obeying those impulses—to pause and receive rest and nurture from God. When the idolatries of our world (for example, money, pleasure, and power) invite our allegiance, sabbath invites us to focus a full day on worshiping the one God.

I'm indebted to Eugene Peterson for helping me connect sabbath to the Hebrew sense of beginning with rest. Peterson notes that the Hebrew day begins at sundown and embodies a life of trusting God. In this rhythm, we begin our time with nourishment and rest, believing that God is doing the foundational work of restoration and growth. Then we wake and add our own efforts to participate in God's good work. This pattern shines out as especially poignant for those working in agriculture. While the farmer sleeps and rises, God provides the miracle of growth. Though the farmer participates with hard work by the sweat of her brow, the fruit is still a miracle. Peterson makes the point that sabbath keeping allows us to follow the same

pattern with our weekly rhythm. We rest and worship, then we enter
into the work God has prepared. In contrast, if we never stop working,
we live out the anxious toil of our culture. Our actions of constant
busyness teach our souls to worship productivity and self-reliance. We
need fundamental disciplines of *stopping* our work in order to become
people of faith, hope, and love.

In his Gospel, Luke emphasizes that same pattern of starting with
rest and prayer. Jesus' ministry begins with trinitarian love in the
baptism, just as the Hebrew day begins with nourishment and rest.
Jesus' redemptive work begins with receiving identity, affection, and
pleasure from the Father, just as our week begins with sabbath rest
and worship.

Looking at the narrative of Luke from a wide-angle lens, we can see
distinctive Hebrew rhythms. We see the annual Jewish patterns as
Jesus is circumcised on the eighth day and as his family travels to the
festival when he is twelve. Through the middle of Luke, we see Jesus
in alternating scenes of action and prayer. When sabbath specifically
comes up in Luke, Jesus critiques legalism but maintains a faithful
sabbath practice and emphasizes its importance.

Earlier I introduced a list of disciplines that help me seek God in
the cultivated wilderness of consecration. Sabbath is the most fundamental of these disciplines. We pause and find nourishment. We allow
God to form us in identity, affection, and pleasure. In addition to
weekly sabbath, I find I need monthly and annual patterns as well. But
they all follow the pattern of sabbath. When I create space to rest and
pray, the shape of my life teaches my soul to trust God. And this is not
some glorious mystical spiral of improvement! For me the practices of
daily prayer, sabbath, and periodic retreat feel more remedial, like I'm
being re-educated through repentance, forgiveness, and a fresh invitation to trust. I need formation apart from work, because my interface
with the world, the flesh, and the devil are always deforming my soul
and spoiling the goodness of the work.

RETREAT AS A SABBATH EXPERIENCE

Lake Winnebago in central Wisconsin spans such a distance that you can't see from one side to the other. It is a beautiful body of water surrounded by woods and hills. The lake's name originates from the local Ho-Chunk Native American tribe. The small cities of Oshkosh and Fond du Lac occupy the western and southern shores of the lake. Between these two cities lies the Jesuit Retreat House where my team takes an annual weeklong Ignatian silent retreat.

In the summer of 2023, I arrived for retreat grumpy and exhausted, with dark circles under my eyes. In my emotionally depleted state, I wondered whether my life of ministry would be sustainable. The past year had involved a great deal of conflict, emotional pain, and deep disappointment. My heart and soul had run dry. I could tell my reserves were gone, because relatively small issues were causing enormous swings of emotion for me. I had been waking up regularly in the night, fuming with anger or crumpled with despair.

As a pastoral leader, I'm supposed to be the guy who takes everything in stride, giving comfort to others while I help the whole community move forward. That mojo had flown out the window for me and my heart was in chaos. I came to retreat desperate for discernment and renewal. Before retreat, I wrote to my intercessor team (the small team that prays intensely for me), asking them to pray for three requests: that I would clearly diagnose the damaged state of my soul, that I would be able to repent of any idolatry that contributed to my state, and that I would discern any implications for my coming year of ministry.

My habit on these extended retreats is to pray through Scripture passages each day. Each day I also meet with my spiritual director to discuss how I'm praying, what I'm receiving from God, and what Bible passages I might reflect on. Each afternoon the whole retreat community gathers for a brief Communion service. Within the retreat, these rhythms help keep us focused on prayer and connected to truth and grace.

God always meets me in the Word and brings it alive to me on these retreats. This week was no exception—the Scriptures were rich—but images from nature tied the themes together. The opening night followed a day of heavy rains. Two days before, sixty-mile-an-hour winds had buffeted the retreat grounds, which are covered with beautiful, historic trees. When I walked the path by the lake that first night, I saw a battlefield of broken branches on the ground. Large limbs and entire uprooted trees displayed the power of the wind to snap one trunk like a pencil and leave the next intact. The wind was still blowing hard that night, and the lake was surging with small whitecaps. Father Mark, the director of the Jesuit Retreat House and also my spiritual director, says the lake has a different personality each day. That evening it was stirring and spitting in fits of rage. Somehow the lake's grumpy mood fit my own, so I put on a jacket and sat out on a dock to pray.

The gusts whipped my jacket around me, slapping my face. The wind sucked warmth from my body, but the lake's agitation was strangely comforting, as if it understood the storms I had experienced in the past year. While the lake seemed my companion, my prayers led me to contemplate the trees. What led some of the trees to break and others to survive? In the storms of my own life, what limbs had fallen and what cracks could I recognize on this retreat? Taking in my dark mood, my spiritual director encouraged a more positive viewpoint, asking what were the deep, healthy roots and strong, flexible fibers in the tree of my soul? And what were the roots and strong fibers in my community?

The first full day of the retreat, I prayed through those questions about my soul and my community, considering them like trees. This was not a simple transition in my prayers. It was a challenging day of retreat. I needed to pour out some of my stormy thoughts before God, and I did so while walking and running and journaling. Father Mark assigned me to pray through the beginning of Isaiah 43, and God's tender words there helped me eventually turn the corner into a posture of gratitude. The Holy Spirit encouraged me as I considered deep roots and strong fibers. I felt renewed grief and pain at fallen branches and deep cracks.

As I sought solace from the grief of the past year, Father Mark gently led me to contemplate the love of God. Of course this seems obvious, but I needed the reminder. Often the benefit of a spiritual director in my life is to help me articulate my struggle, then to point me in the obvious direction of God's love. I have found spiritual direction especially helpful in times of confusion and pain. Out of the merciful reflection on God's love, the Spirit convicted me of sin and called me to repentance. I realized that over the past year, I had engaged tensions and grief more through responsibility than through love. As a leader, I needed to hold tension and absorb pain for others in difficult circumstances of conflict and unexpected change. This is, of course, a regular dynamic of leadership. And yet as a follower of Jesus I'm called beyond navigating crises with responsible poise. My high sense of responsibility (number two on my Clifton Strengths, if that means something to you) was keeping me engaged, but I was doing the right things mostly out of duty, with little sense of love.

While I reflected on God's love, the truth slowly soaked into my heart. Contrary to the message of responsibility, I am not the protagonist of the story. I'm called to love those around me with Christ's own love. I'm called to carry pain not with pride and duty but with tender humility—an invitation both vulnerable and painful. From the perspective of leadership responsibility, I'm able to keep a certain distance from the suffering of others. But from the perspective of love, the cost is higher and the pain deeper. And yet, when we love others in the name of Jesus, we also participate in God's love for us and for all of creation. The vulnerability of love is matched by the infinite resources of God's love. Through messy, conflicted prayers and a lot of journaling, I processed these thoughts. I realized I had distanced myself from God's love out of self-protection: "If I move forward only in responsibility, it will hurt less." In my self-protection, I robbed myself and others of love.

So I confessed the sins of depending on myself, hardening my heart, and neglecting love. As I confessed this to Father Mark, he offered me God's forgiveness and an assignment of how to pray for God's love for others on the retreat. I felt God's invitation to move forward without shame.

On retreat, God was inviting me to a sabbath experience with my burdens. As a leader I was carrying others' burdens, and Jesus was assuring me that he was already carrying my burdens and those of the people I love.

The movement of repentance took my retreat from the trees back to the water. My intercessors had been praying for me to become more like a reservoir, based on a quote from Saint Bernard of Clairvaux:

> The man who is wise, therefore, will see his life as more like a reservoir than a canal. The canal simultaneously pours out what it receives; the reservoir retains the water till it is filled, then discharges the overflow without loss to itself. . . . Today there are many in the Church who act like canals, the reservoirs are far too rare. . . . You too must learn to await this fullness before pouring out your gifts, do not try to be more generous than God.

Sitting by the lake, I turned to pray for filling with the love of God. I contemplated Lake Winnebago, which I learned is filled with 2.3 billion cubic meters of water. The weight of that water is over five trillion pounds. Its immensity sat before me as a witness to the nature of fullness. Fullness has mass, volume, substance, and presence. I sat with the weight of the water and felt my soul stabilized by the mass of God's love.

One evening sitting on the dock, the lake was again in a tumult of whitecaps. This time, however, my focus was on the depth and mass and volume of the lake. Gusty winds affect the surface of the water, but over a cubic mile of water rested completely at peace under the surface. I asked that God would fill my soul with a mass and volume of his love so I could love, grieve, and lead deeply and strongly, from the resources of that love. I waited on God, who alone can fill the reservoir of my soul.

With all those sensations, I spent time praying the prayer of Ephesians 3:17-19 for myself and for those I'm called to love—that we, "being rooted and established in love, may have power, together with all the Lord's holy people, to grasp how wide and long and high and deep is the love of Christ, and to know this love that surpasses knowledge— that [we] may be filled to the measure of all the fullness of God."

I returned from the retreat restored and reminded of what I have learned many times—that the love of God is the main thing about my life, about the world, and about the universe.

My sabbath experience on the shores of Lake Winnebago brought about a renewal of baptism. I entered that retreat deformed, depleted, and discouraged by my experiences. God invited me to explore brokenness and sin as well as strength and resilience. But mostly, he invited me to soak in the waters of his love. He poured identity, affection, and pleasure into my heart. I reflected on my baptism, where I was washed and raised up as a member of the body of Jesus—the same body that was immersed in the Jordan all those years ago. Sitting by the lake, I felt the immensity of the baptismal waters of the universal church. The love of God is so massive that it has washed and redeemed his people from history past through eternity future.

As a leader, I find myself in need of baptism renewal on a regular basis. The stress of my calling tends to activate the toxic parts of my family and identities, and it takes me away from the love and pleasure of God. I'm grateful that Jesus' baptism consistently invites me back to the water. The baptism icon hangs in a prayer room in my house and draws me to Luke 3 on a daily basis. In prayer I am washed, renewed, and enfolded in the redeemed people of God.

Some of us (especially leaders) are tempted to work ceaselessly. Some of us are also tempted to rest thoughtlessly, expecting that entertainment or avoidance will fill us up. Sabbath is intentional, both as a pause from work and an engagement with God. In that intentionality, sabbath keeping is leadership. Sabbath disciplines are radical. They direct my attention to the roots of my life. At the root level, I draw nutrition and pure water from God's truth and love. I also sink roots deeply into the soil below me, gaining stability for times when storms may threaten to topple me. Sabbath disciplines also shape my radical, revolutionary posture in the world. By stopping and praying, I turn my life away from the powers and principalities that use people and toil for the sake of money, pleasure, and power. By pausing and intentionally seeking God, I center my life on the identity, affection, and pleasure that only God can speak over me.

PRACTICE: DEVELOP A SABBATH ROUTINE

Sabbath keeping is a habit to learn and cultivate. I encourage you to take several weeks and try different practices. Reflect on each different sabbath experience and note what seemed deepening and life-giving to you. Then keep adjusting your routine—keeping a few simple practices that help you enter into God's life-giving presence.

Here are a few suggestions in establishing a sabbath practice:

- Reserve the same time each week if possible. Twenty-four hours is helpful, but especially for parents of young children, a shorter time may be more realistic. It doesn't have to be Saturday or Sunday.

- Try beginning your sabbath with a ritual of some sort that represents stopping work and devoting yourself to God. In Jewish custom, the sabbath begins with lighting a candle, praying a prayer, and speaking a blessing over each member of the family. Your ritual could be very simple, like lighting a candle and reading a psalm.

- Explore what activities are energizing to you and what brings you closer to God. Choose from that list.

- Consider solitude and community. What mix of those two will be restorative to you? Also consider what members of your community need to know about your sabbath because they are impacted by it.

- Consider place—is there a part of your home or community that helps you relax? Is there a place that you should avoid because it causes you stress?

- Try also ending your sabbath with a particular prayer or Scripture, and use the same one for a few weeks in a row.

For more learning, some sabbath resources:

Lynne Baab, *Sabbath Keeping* (Downers Grove, IL: InterVarsity Press, 2005).

Ruth Haley Barton, *Embracing Rhythms of Work and Rest* (Downers Grove, IL: InterVarsity Press, 2022), particularly chapters 1–8.

Walter Brueggemann, *Sabbath as Resistance*, rev. ed. (Louisville: Westminster John Knox, 2017).

Marva Dawn, *Keeping the Sabbath Wholly* (Grand Rapids, MI: Eerdmans, 1989).

Abraham Joshua Heschel, *The Sabbath* (New York: Farrar, Straus and Giroux, 1951).

6

CHARACTER FORMATION

Tested in the Wilderness

Holy Spirit, please help us follow your lead into the wilderness where you shape our character to be more like Jesus. Show us how to recognize and choose this formation that seems mundane but also holds great spiritual power. Form and purify our identities by your Word and through our communities.

My family was strangely entertained by character formation. It came from my dad. He was born with a clubfoot in 1933, and his mom managed to get a ticket by train from their small farm in North Dakota to the Mayo Clinic in Minnesota. There, as an infant, he received basic surgery (cutting-edge at the time) to turn his foot from facing backward to forward. Though that leg was disfigured and weak for his whole life, Dad figured out how to work through pain and thrive as an athlete, a farm hand, a husband and father, and a businessman.

Surviving the pain shaped him. His personality, character, and heart were different because of his journey. Later as a family, we would half joke in the face of any suffering that "it builds character." We also joked that Amos 3:2 should be our family verse:

You only have I chosen
    of all the families of the earth;
therefore I will punish you
    for all your sins.

Yes, that's pretty intense, but we were highlighting the positive growth that can come through suffering. I'm grateful for the lightheartedness of our joking, which demonstrated a security of love in the family. I also thank God that suffering can indeed help build character.

Mature Christian leadership, as we've seen, is marked by a paradoxical combination of tender humility and bold faith. The humility-plus-faith connection helps us grow as disciples while we follow God's call to serve as leaders. It balances our roots with our branches, our depth with our reach. Unfortunately, we don't naturally embody humility and faith. Our character bends naturally toward arrogance and fear. We need constant formation as we seek to grow in both identity and calling.

Character formation is the process by which we see ourselves more clearly, grow in the fruit of the Spirit, and increasingly embody the identity and calling that God gives us. We become more like Jesus and more like our true selves. The process lasts for our whole lives.

THE MESSIAH'S FIRST FORTY DAYS

Beginnings are important in leadership. In politics, we watch the first one hundred days of a presidency to see the agenda and effectiveness of a new administration. Leadership-themed bookstore shelves (or internet searches) are full of bestselling titles like *The New Leader's 100 Day Action Plan* and the shockingly reduced *The First 90 Days*. A leader's first choices and moves say a lot about her values.

As Christian leaders, we should pay special attention to the beginning of the newly anointed Messiah's time in office. As I've mentioned, the terms *Messiah* and *Christ* literally refer to "the anointed one." So when Jesus dramatically receives the Spirit at his baptism, it is his public coronation as Messiah. His administration begins there by the Jordan. The Spirit anoints Jesus as Messiah. What immediately follows is startling.

> Jesus, full of the Holy Spirit, left the Jordan and was led by the
> Spirit into the wilderness, where for forty days he was tempted

by the devil. He ate nothing during those days, and at the end of
them he was hungry. (Luke 4:1-2)

Jesus the Messiah's first move is to follow. Jesus is full of the Spirit,
but rather than wielding the Spirit's power like a weapon, he is led and
he follows. Second, Jesus goes into the wilderness (rather than the
city). Third, Jesus engages testing. Finally, he practices disciplined
restraint by fasting. Those are not the distinctives I often hear about
in a new president's first hundred days! Let's look more deeply into
Jesus' beginning.

Jesus followed. He was both "full of the Spirit" and "led by the
Spirit." How do you think that worked for him? The text does not tell
us precisely how Jesus discerned and followed the Spirit. However,
context, imagination, and experience can help us. Theological and
biblical context tells us the Holy Spirit is a person, equal and coeternal
with Jesus and the Father. So Jesus' relationship with the Spirit is not
like listening to the mysterious voice in *Field of Dreams* or meeting the
creepy ghosts in *A Christmas Carol*. It's mysterious, but it's not about
a magical voice.

I think Jesus experienced the Spirit in his humanness. Jesus per-
ceived and followed the Spirit's lead much like we do—through a mysterious mix of mind, body, emotions, and will. It is a complex and
organic process. Trying to imagine his experience, I speculate that he
felt the love and truth poured out on him from the Father through the
Spirit—a deep sense of peace and affection, of pure, holy love. Jesus
had been immersed in the Law and Prophets of the Old Testament. We
see this immersion in his twelve-year-old experience in the temple in
Luke 2. I suspect that in the baptism, he experienced his mind filled
with the Scriptures he had studied, and his gut-level will or desire inclined him to worship God in the wilderness.

Jesus the Lord of all paused enough to pay attention to the Spirit's
leading, and he humbled himself enough to follow. The fact that the
Spirit led him suggests that left to his own sensibilities, he might have

done something else. He might have moved forward in the urgency of his mission. But Jesus began by listening and following, and he calls us to do the same.

The Spirit leads Jesus to the wilderness first. Not to the city for a Messiah rally or even to gather his messianic cabinet for a strategy session. Why might that be? There are two major reasons revealed by the biblical narrative. First, Jesus is faithfully reliving the narrative of Israel called out of oppression to become God's own people. The Old Testament story consistently presents the exodus journey as a meta-narrative for God's people. God brings Israel through a formative experience in the wilderness, and in the process he teaches them to no longer be slaves but rather to be his treasured children.

The exodus story also looks forward to the Messiah completing this narrative in the ultimate liberation of God's people. As we look closely at the devil's temptations and Jesus' responses in Luke 4, we see that Jesus is reflecting on Deuteronomy and the ways God's people were not faithful to him when they came out of Egypt. In each temptation, Jesus responds with a text from Deuteronomy. Jesus is reliving that narrative with faithfulness, in line with his calling. Like Israel, Jesus goes for testing and identity formation in the wilderness before entering the promised land of the kingdom of God to free his people. But Jesus is faithful where Israel was not.

Second, Jesus goes to the wilderness to accomplish important work in the spiritual realm. Matthew 12, Mark 3, and Luke 11 all record an interaction in which Jesus references a strong man being bound and the strong man's house being plundered. In each case Jesus is referring to his work casting out demons, healing, and forgiving people. Looking at the Gospel narratives to see when the strong man (Satan) is bound, we therefore need to check when his house (of demons) begins to be plundered. In each account this happens when Jesus returns from the wilderness. In each Gospel we can deduce that the devil is bound through Jesus' faithful journey of testing. Jesus' first move to the wilderness reveals his values of reestablishing Israel's faithful identity and of binding the spiritual power of the enemy.

Similarly, one of our first priorities in living out our calling as disciples and leaders is to establish faithfulness in the story of our life. Rather than sprinting forward in productivity, we follow Jesus by pausing and considering our own growth in character and spiritual authority.

In the wilderness, Jesus engages the temptations of the devil. He does not avoid or deny them. In fact, the Spirit seems to lead Jesus into the wilderness for that very purpose. This surprises me, because I often assume an incremental approach to growth—that we address our issues not immediately, but eventually—when we have no other choice. Perhaps for me that represents avoidance of conflict and tension. Jesus shows no such avoidance. With courage he follows the Spirit's lead into a place of danger and vulnerability. He is willing to engage silence, solitude, and fasting. These require a particular kind of courage.

He is brave enough to face the devil's attack at the level of his deepest temptations. I'm not saying Jesus went to the wilderness looking for the devil, in search of temptation. The parallel with the exodus story indicates he went into the wilderness (following the Spirit's lead) in order to worship. But just like the Israelites, Jesus engages temptation in the journey to worship. By going to the wilderness in solitude and fasting, he demonstrates the priority of facing his temptations and allowing the Spirit to shape his character. He doesn't wait until after the first ninety or hundred days of his Messiah administration. Rather, he prioritizes the refinement of his character, the testing of his faith, and the purification of his worship. Jesus' union with the Father through the Spirit is that important. His character is that important. And his overcoming of the enemy is that important.

Jesus begins his leadership with restraint, through fasting. Not with bluster or showing off, but alone, unseen, and disciplined. I see few leadership communications (Christian or non-Christian) that promote fasting as a leadership activity. Yet it is the first thing Jesus does as Messiah. He chooses to discipline his appetites in pursuit of worship.

He prioritizes integrity over assertion. He shows assertiveness later in his leadership journey, but Jesus' first moves show us that his truth flows from integrity tested in the furnace of disciplined abstinence.

For us, there is no better time than the present to address our most challenging temptations. We gain nothing by avoiding or denying them. We are shaped as much by what we choose *not* to do as we are by what we choose to do. We can choose disciplines that curb or tame our most problematic appetites, whether those are media consumption, attention seeking, or any other self-centering indulgence. The spiritual and moral battle for holiness is the most critical battle in our life and our leadership.

THE TEMPTATIONS

The particular temptations and Jesus' responses provide lessons in leadership formation. In these reflections I'm especially indebted to Henri Nouwen's book *In the Name of Jesus.*

The first temptation is beautifully poetic and sets the stage for all three. Jesus is hungry (of course, after fasting for forty days), and the devil says, "Tell this stone to become bread." Jesus immediately replies from Deuteronomy 8: "Man shall not live on bread alone" (Luke 4:3-4). The people of Israel were tested in the wilderness, as recorded in Exodus. In Deuteronomy, Moses is looking back and reflecting on those forty years of testing. Here's the passage Jesus quotes, in context:

> Remember how the LORD your God led you all the way in the wilderness these forty years, to humble and test you in order to know what was in your heart, whether or not you would keep his commands. He humbled you, causing you to hunger and then feeding you with manna, which neither you nor your ancestors had known, to teach you that man does not live on bread alone but on every word that comes from the mouth of the LORD. Your clothes did not wear out and your feet did not swell during these forty years. Know then in your heart that as a man

disciplines his son, so the LORD your God disciplines you. (Deuteronomy 8:2-5)

What a great first exchange this is between Jesus and the devil—as if the pugilists are testing one another's defenses! Appetite is at stake, and also identity. Note that in Deuteronomy, the Lord is working on more than just physical provision for his people. Rather, he is shaping their identity as his children. Jesus in turn is reflecting on Deuteronomy to explore his own identity after his baptism. The devil offers the chance for Jesus to provide for himself, satisfying his own appetites. But Jesus recognizes that the hunger of the wilderness, according to Deuteronomy, is meant to humble God's people and lead them to attach more deeply to the Lord. In his hunger, Jesus resolves to "feed" on the Word by reflecting on Deuteronomy and trusting the Father. In this way he passes the wilderness test where Israel failed it by complaining in Exodus 16–17.

Jesus' intentional fasting accomplishes at least two things. First, fasting brings self-awareness. In fasting Jesus allows his appetite or hunger to be revealed. He is honest and fully dependent on God in his embodied, human, hungry state. We all have our hungry needs, but we are often blind to both those needs and the compulsive ways we fill them. I have found that fasting helps reveal my appetites, not only for food but also for other fulfillments. Only when I fast from food or entertainment or news do I really learn how much I have depended on that commodity to manage my life. When I fast, the Spirit invites me to worship God and depend on him more fully.

Second, Jesus intentionally feeds on the Word while abstaining from food. By engaging deeply with the Scriptures, he fulfills the message of Deuteronomy 8. And through the Word, God offers Jesus clear identity and escape from temptation. Fasting as simply abstaining from food is of some value to prayer, but when combined with feasting on the Word, it is transformative.

We can ask the Holy Spirit to speak to us about the appetites that control us. And then, like Jesus, we can try fasting and learn more about our hunger. If we pair that discipline of abstinence with feasting on Scripture, it can be a powerful combination for our growth.

In the second temptation, the devil offers Jesus authority and splendor in exchange for worship. I'm fascinated that the tempter is so transparent about offering something that is not his creation but rather has been given to him. Authority and splendor have been abdicated by sinful people and cultures, given to the devil as we fall to temptation.

Again, Jesus sees through the deception by reflecting on Deuteronomy. His response is from Deuteronomy 6:13: "Worship the Lord your God and serve him only" (Luke 4:8). Jesus recognizes that if he accepts the authority and splendor offered to him, it will be ascribed, given by another under temptation, not gained with integrity. Jesus chooses the integrity of worshiping the one true God rather than receiving by shortcut or deception. Henri Nouwen reads this as the temptation to be spectacular or popular. Jesus refuses such shallow rewards in favor of the more permanent and intrinsic rewards of the authority that comes from true integrity and the splendor of holiness.

In this temptation I also see a reflection of Israel's long journey in the wilderness. It took a long time for God's people to learn not to be slaves any longer. There were no shortcuts to enter the Promised Land. Likewise, by refusing a shortcut, Jesus showed his willingness to follow God's timing. He was willing to gain authority at the slow pace of integrity rather than the accelerated pace of spectacle.

Many of us are attracted to appearing spectacular, popular, or successful, and we may be willing to get those things by any means necessary. Yet if we pursue these things with abandon, we compromise our integrity and subtly ascribe our worship to something other than God. Consider inviting the Spirit to speak to you about any situations where you may be trading your true worship for something cheaper.

In the third temptation, the devil lures Jesus toward proving his own identity. The devil seems to be searching for insecurity and fear in Jesus. The tempter says, "If you are the Son of God . . . ," offering a challenge to Jesus' identity spoken by the Father at his baptism. By taking Jesus to the temple, the devil engages the most important symbol of the Lord's presence. And then he quotes Scripture, noting the Lord's promise in Psalm 91:11-12 that angels would bear him up and keep him from harm. The devil is saying, "Prove it! Let everyone know who you are!" Jesus' response, however, continues to flow from his reflection on Deuteronomy. His response, "Do not put the Lord your God to the test" (Luke 4:12), comes from Deuteronomy 6:16: "Do not put the LORD your God to the test as you did at Massah."

Massah means "testing." The Israelites were thirsty and complained against Moses, saying, "Why did you bring us up out of Egypt to make us and our children and livestock die of thirst?" (Exodus 17:3). But in the larger context of Exodus 16–17, their testing of the Lord was that they looked and complained to Moses and Aaron rather than looking to the Lord. Exodus 16:6-8 says:

> So Moses and Aaron said to all the Israelites, "In the evening you will know that it was the LORD who brought you out of Egypt, and in the morning you will see the glory of the LORD, because he has heard your grumbling against him. Who are we, that you should grumble against us?" Moses also said, "You will know that it was the LORD when he gives you meat to eat in the evening and all the bread you want in the morning, because he has heard your grumbling against him. Who are we? You are not grumbling against us, but against the LORD."

The Israelites failed the test of Massah because in their insecurity, they looked to the wrong source for provision. Later they similarly look to the wrong source by making a golden calf.

Jesus discerns that the devil's invitation is probing for insecurity, tempting him to gain his identity from the wrong source. Instead,

Jesus trusts his identity in the Father and refuses to prove himself. My own consistent temptation is to consider my work as the source of my identity rather than God. Especially when I have failed or received critique, I feel the compulsion to work harder in order to prove my value. When I pause and reflect in a moment like that, I recognize that the compulsive work is an attempt to cover my sadness, insecurity, or anger.

We are all tempted to prove our identity in various ways. We can, however, ask the Holy Spirit to show us these temptations and lead us toward integrity, security, and wholeness. These healthy qualities will lead us to worship and also empower our leadership.

When the Spirit leads Jesus into the wilderness, the Spirit also draws him to reflect specifically on Deuteronomy. Jesus sits with Moses' reflections on the people of God in the wilderness. As he prepares to proclaim the kingdom of God, Jesus soaks in God's words about his wandering people being tested before entering the Promised Land. In Jesus' character formation, Scripture is his clear source of truth and authority. And so it should be for us. The living and authoritative Word of God is our compass and our true north as we navigate temptation and allow God to shape our character.

CHARACTER FORMATION AND DISCIPLESHIP GROWTH

Just as he led Jesus, the Spirit leads us into the wilderness to shape our character. Just as we need to consistently return to our baptism to find ourselves beloved, chosen, and cleansed, we also need to return to the wilderness of testing again and again over the course of our lives.

When we find ourselves in challenging circumstances, we always have an opportunity to grow. God loves to appear in the wilderness of our experience. Challenges reveal our appetites and temptations. They offer us the opportunity to trust God more deeply and worship him more fully.

We must follow Jesus' example, imitating his move to follow the Spirit into the wilderness in fasting and prayer. We feed on the Word and allow the Spirit to shape our hearts. Disciplines of abstinence (like fasting, solitude, and silence) shape us. They reveal and curb our appetites. They allow us to create space for prayer and Scripture. They help us let go of the ways we manipulate ourselves and our world. They help us listen and look to God, but they also bring our temptations to light.

As a person who makes a living by talking to other people, I have come to realize that extended silences help me let go of my addiction to spoken words and listen for the quiet voice of the Spirit. When I fast from food, my irritability rises to the surface and allows me to examine and repent of critical attitudes. I love tea and take joy in brewing and drinking it every day—but I take an extended fast from caffeine once a year and often discover God speaking to me about how I treat my body and manage my energy. The Spirit uses all of these to open me up to the Word and give me opportunities to grow.

God shapes us in cooperation with our own initiative. Though God is the potter and we are the clay, we are not passive participants in our formation. The Spirit is often leading us into the wilderness, but we choose whether to pay attention and follow. When we are suffering, we choose whether to seek the Lord's discipline and guidance in the midst of it. When we have the opportunity, we choose whether to practice disciplines that will contribute to our formation. When we expect God to form us through suffering and discipline, we can then soak in the Word for healing and help.

Let me suggest one simple process. Ask the Lord how he might want to shape your character, and also ask someone else who knows you well how God might want to grow your character. If helpful, consider the fruit of the Spirit in Galatians 5:22-23. When you have a sense of what God may want to do, then ask God how you might cooperate in that process. Consider asking a friend something like, "I think God wants me to grow in patience (or another fruit). How do you think I might actively cooperate with the Spirit in that process?"

CHARACTER FORMATION, LEADERSHIP,
AND SPIRITUAL WARFARE

Chances are, the idea of spiritual warfare freaks you out a little bit. It can feel either distant and irrelevant or sinister and fearful. For those of us who naturally avoid conflict, even if we believe spiritual warfare is real, we pretend it doesn't exist. Because of Scripture, some of us believe in spiritual conflict but try to keep it as theoretical as possible. Others have real experiences with evil or spiritual powers but feel unequipped to deal with them. Some (especially from Catholic, charismatic, and Pentecostal traditions) have received teaching about deliverance, but even in those communities there can be confusion and fear. My goal here is to address one small but central area in that larger subject—the area that flows from Luke 4. Spiritual warfare is real and relevant to discipleship and leadership. But spiritual authority is gained through the mundane work of character formation.

Jesus bound the devil through his faithfulness under testing in the wilderness. He experienced fasting, prayer, feeding on the Word, choosing faithful worship, and clarifying his identity. Somehow all of those seemingly private experiences had power in the spiritual realm and affected his leadership immediately. Luke 4:14 says, "Jesus returned to Galilee in the power of the Spirit" and goes on to describe the power of his ministry.

In our own limited way, we, too, return from the wilderness in the power of the Spirit. Jesus is the one who ultimately bound the devil, but we gain spiritual authority through the work of character formation. A leader receives vision and calling, and there are spiritual forces that will oppose every holy calling from God. I'm convinced these evil spiritual forces are real. I have seen dramatic spiritual warfare and deliverance from demonic oppression. However, this book is not mainly about that drama.

Instead it's about grasping the truth that our identity, character, and integrity are the front line of spiritual warfare. Spiritual opposition poses a danger not only to your soul but to your leadership calling, and victories in the wilderness of temptation are victories for both. To the extent that you grow in holiness and integrity, you also grow in the spiritual authority to do good and defeat evil.

I was in my midthirties when I was invited to co-lead intercessory prayer for the Urbana missions conference. The assignment seemed huge to me, yet I felt clearly called to accept. Prayer at previous Urbana conferences had involved dramatic spiritual conflict, and it was led by people older and more mature than I was. I felt that the spiritual burden of leading this prayer effort was beyond what I could carry— like I had agreed to wrestle someone far above my weight class. So I asked my spiritual director Father Tom to suggest disciplines that might prepare me for the challenge ahead. Father Tom prayed a bit, smiled, and told me, "You need to learn to pray the stations of the cross." I hadn't seen that coming!

So I did research, learned as much as I could, and started to practice this traditional method of worshiping Jesus in his Passion. I spent over a year cultivating this discipline, and I was shocked by how fruitful it was for my growth. I learned to worship Jesus in his suffering, in his humility, in his faith, and in his love. I found myself changed as I lingered with Christ as he was judged, tortured, and betrayed. The Spirit revealed my pride, impatience, triumphalism, and avoidance of pain, and I worshiped the Lord in his holiness.

When the conference arrived, I found I had what I needed to be faithful in the experiences of spiritual warfare. Even in some dramatic prayer encounters, I experienced spiritual authority through the paradox of worshiping Jesus in his humility and willing sacrifice. By God's grace, my formation led to spiritual victory in that leadership experience.

As Jesus' baptism invites us to formation at the level of our being (beloved children, chosen and pleasurable), so Jesus' temptation invites us to formation in our character development—our becoming.

PRACTICE: FASTING

Fasting is not punishment and should never be performative (see Matthew 6:16-18). Rather, fasting is an embodiment of prayer. In fasting we choose to abstain from something for a period of time in order to discipline our appetites and focus on God. We allow certain hungers to increase, and with that we express our hunger for God. We hunger and thirst for God like the deer in Psalm 42:1.

I invite you to choose a period of time for fasting and to choose what you will abstain from. Most people fast from food, but this is not healthy for some. Many choose to fast from their phone, from a particular kind of food, from caffeine, or from certain activities like small talk or critique.

Along with your chosen fast, focus on your intention for the fast. Are you seeking increased intimacy with God? Are you praying for cleansing and holiness in a particular area of life? Are you asking God for a word of discernment or direction? Choose one main prayer as your focus for the fast.

Spend a dedicated time of prayer (even very brief) at the beginning and end of your fast. Express your intention, commit yourself to God, and listen for a while. Sometimes the Lord surprises us and speaks or moves differently from our intention, but often he will speak to our intentions. God promises to meet us and shape us as we fast.

Go about your business during the time of the fast. When your hunger arises, remember that this is your body praying your intentions to God. If you make a mistake or fail in your fast, ask God for mercy and have mercy on yourself as well. Confess and move on.

I recommend journaling at the end of your fast. Simply write about your intention, your experience, and any ways the Lord may have met you, spoken to you, or changed you.

GROUP GUIDE 4

Read Luke 4:1-13 aloud. Note the cross-referenced texts in the passage: Deuteronomy 8:3; Deuteronomy 6:13; Psalm 91:11-12; Deuteronomy 6:16.

Observe

- What repeated words or themes do you notice in the story?
- Imagining the story as a movie, what do you notice in the scenes? What might the theme music be like for these scenes?

Interpret

- What questions arise for you from this story?
- Why do you think these particular temptations were offered and not others?
- What do you think is the significance of Jesus' particular responses from Deuteronomy?
- Why do you think the Spirit led Jesus into this experience?

Apply

- If the Spirit led you individually into the wilderness to face off with the devil, what temptations do you think the devil would choose?
- What do you think are the core temptations for your group or team right now?
- What passage of Scripture might God be giving you (as a group or individual) to respond to temptations in this season?

GROUP DISCUSSION QUESTIONS FOR
CHAPTERS 5-6 (30 MINUTES)

Radical rest

1. What are the rhythms of rest and replenishment in your life currently?

2. What are those rhythms in your group or team?

3. In the discussion of sabbath and other patterns of rest, what stood out to you as attractive?

4. In what ways do you resist rest, and why?

Testing

5. If you were in the first hundred days of your leadership right now, what would be your top priorities and goals?

6. In light of those priorities, what do you think and feel about Jesus' first days as publicly anointed Messiah?

7. In what area do you think God currently wants to shape your character? How might God bring about that shaping?

8. What do you think spiritual authority looks like for you personally?

9. What does spiritual authority look like in your group or team?

SPIRITUAL AUTHORITY AND CHRISTIAN LEADERSHIP

JESUS WENT INTO THE WILDERNESS "full of the Holy Spirit," and he returned from the wilderness "in the power of the Spirit" (Luke 4:1, 14). Later when he preached in the synagogue, people remarked, "What words these are! With authority and power he gives orders to impure spirits and they come out!" (Luke 4:36).

How can we understand the mysterious quality of spiritual authority? Since we're not Jesus, how is it even possible to embody the authority of the Spirit? I have seen and experienced a lot of confusion in this area, so I'll offer a few clarifiers here.

WHAT SPIRITUAL AUTHORITY IS

Spiritual authority is integrity—not charisma. Sometimes we want to measure spiritual authority by the impressiveness of someone's gifts or by their personal charisma. Scripture seems to say, however, that true spiritual authority comes from character. Charm and power of personality can be counterfeit, but the Spirit works in the deep formation of our souls and establishes a base of authority there. Humility is a marker of true spiritual authority, and pride is a marker of its absence.

Spiritual authority is love—not authoritarianism. Beware of those who claim spiritual authority over others or exercise a form of "executive privilege." Often this is a tragic form of abuse. Jesus shows us that spiritual authority leads us to lay down our lives in love for others. We develop spiritual authority as we practice following Jesus by loving and serving those around us and praying for our enemies.

Spiritual authority is holiness—not pragmatism. Successful leadership does not necessarily point to spiritual authority. God brings success or failure where God chooses, and sometimes he uses profoundly broken and bent people to accomplish holy and beautiful things. Beware of those who use success to claim spiritual authority. Judging from Jesus' life, true authority in the Spirit sometimes produces miraculous results, but it also produces suffering, rejection, and death. Spiritual authority is a measure of our congruence with the will and Word of God, not a measure of effectiveness.

WHAT SPIRITUAL AUTHORITY DOES

Spiritual authority embodies the kingdom of God. Integrity, love, and holiness create a culture and dynamic around people. When leaders practice these traits, the community begins to live out the kingdom of God. When leaders embody integrity, others are more likely to forgive one another and speak the truth. When leaders love and serve those around them, especially the marginalized, others begin to trust and follow more willingly. When we see holiness prioritized over results, healthy human dynamics replace some toxic ones. These are more than just sociological dynamics, because the Spirit fills and empowers integrity, love, and holiness and uses them to reveal the mystery of the kingdom breaking into our world.

Spiritual authority prays. Spiritual authority is always embodied in prayer. It's not a superpower to be wielded by a super individual, like lightning rays from the fingers. Rather, spiritual authority is dependence on God to do what God does. We ask Jesus to bind the enemy; we don't bind Satan ourselves. Spiritual authority is another name for praying "in the name of Jesus." When we live and pray in his name, we do so in full unity with his will and presence in the world, and our prayers are filled with his power.

Spiritual authority overcomes spiritual resistance. When leaders are marked by integrity, love, and holiness, the dehumanizing demonic forces in our world are overcome. This doesn't always look like victory to the world, and it never looks like triumphalism (which would be pride). Sometimes the fruit of spiritual authority is subtle, showing up in small miracles of forgiveness, justice, and reconciliation. Sometimes the fruit is impressive and global. I think of historic revivals born out of humble prayer movements, as well as global miracles like the dismantling of apartheid in South Africa.

7

LEADERSHIP CALLING

Entering Nazareth

Lord Jesus, when you entered Nazareth you seemed to know exactly where to be and what to do. We want to know our calling as well! Please grant us the grace to recognize how your Spirit is leading us and the courage to align ourselves with your invitation day by day and over our whole lifetime.

Sometimes God speaks in unexpected ways. Here are three examples of how I've experienced God's calling.

One January while working as a campus minister at UC Berkeley, for the first time I had the overwhelming sense of a "word from the Lord" that I was supposed to deliver to a group of students. I had preached before, but this time I felt like the Spirit had anointed me for this particular message. I identified with the prophet Jeremiah's "burning in my bones" to deliver the word. Because of that sense, I preached with greater boldness and freedom. Multiple students came to faith through that event, and I took great joy in God's faithfulness.

One evening I sat in a group as a wise mentor led us in a discussion about ministry and calling. By the end of the discussion I burst into tears because I realized without a doubt that God was calling me out of that particular group, to move and minister in a different place. The tears represented my grief in leaving the current community but also a great confidence that God was leading me into deeper growth in a particular way. That sense of calling helped me through a difficult period of transition.

Another time Susi and I were desperate to find rental housing in a difficult market. We were living on other people's floors and couches for an extended time, praying hard for God to provide. One day as we were gathered with a small group, we paused for a period of listening prayer, and Susi had a dramatic vision of the scene from Luke 5 where Jesus provides a great catch of fish and calls Peter to follow him. With the group we felt strongly that the Spirit was inviting us to continue following Jesus (by praying and looking for housing), trusting that God would provide what we needed as we "put out into deep water, and let down the nets for a catch" (Luke 5:4). Our faith was strengthened, and within a month God had miraculously provided a house for us. The day after we moved into the house, we learned we were pregnant with our first child. We lived in that house for twenty-four years.

I have experienced a number of moments like these, marked by a powerful sense of God's specific calling, direction, or empowerment. Each time my confidence and faith rise. I identify in those moments with Luke's description of Jesus returning to Galilee "in the power of the Spirit" (Luke 4:14). However, I often struggle for an inspiring sense of God's calling on my whole life. Daily doses of calling are often clear—like the Spirit's invitation to obey the law or give generously to someone we meet in need. But the big pieces are sometimes elusive.

For example, for close to two years now I have felt a growing sense of depletion, and I've not known what to do about it in the big-picture sense. I've practiced all my basic disciplines: rest, guard my times of prayer and play, stay connected to community, ask for prayer. All of these things have helped, but I've felt like a car with a rapidly shrinking gas tank. I need to fill up more and more often and find myself frequently sputtering on fumes. I've asked the Lord what he is doing and how I might move out of this season, and I'm not getting a clear answer. I feel close to God, and I am finding inspiration and guidance in Scripture and moments of joy in community and mission.

I'm just not getting clarity on my current big question about the depletion of my energy.

Sometimes we don't get the "big calling" answers we wish for, but we can still discern and follow God's call. Those big calling questions are important. What particular Scripture should define the shape of my life? What next step am I called to take in my work? With whom am I called to share my life? We all long to know more of the will of God for our lives. We wish for clarity, and we worry about making wrong decisions. It is important to acknowledge the tension and complexity here. We, as imperfect disciples and leaders, will always long for more clarity in our calling. There is no simple formula to know it completely. Yet we can grow in discernment and discover calling in small and large ways.

Pay attention to your longings! Our desire for calling is a desire from God. It is possible to discern God's will in the messy reality of our lives. Looking at the dynamics of Jesus' Nazareth moment in Luke 4 will help us learn to discern the Spirit's invitations in our lives day to day and year to year.

JESUS' ISAIAH 61 CALLING

After his time of testing in the wilderness, Jesus returns to Galilee in the power of the Spirit and the people are amazed: "News about him spread through the whole countryside. He was teaching in their synagogues, and everyone praised him" (Luke 4:14-15). Luke does not say exactly why people are spreading the news. Perhaps they were talking about his dramatic baptism. Perhaps Jesus' face glowed after his encounter with the Father and the Spirit in the Jordan, like Moses' face glowed when he came down from the mountain. Perhaps the people noted that he was gaunt after a forty-day fast! Luke summarizes Jesus' distinctiveness simply as a return "in the power of the Spirit."

When Jesus arrives at the synagogue in Nazareth, he makes clear that he has discerned content and direction for his calling as Messiah. Jesus quotes Isaiah 61:1-2 saying the Spirit is upon him, anointing him (presumably as Messiah) for a specific purpose: to preach good news to the poor, proclaim freedom for the prisoners and recovery of sight for the blind, to set the oppressed free, and to proclaim the year of the Lord's favor. Jesus chooses these specific verses from Isaiah (Luke 4:17-18), then claims, "Today this scripture is fulfilled in your hearing" (Luke 4:21).

Luke shows that the Holy Spirit is active in a variety of ways in Jesus' life. We have noted that his anointing with the Spirit ministered to him at the level of his very being, confirming the identity, affection, and pleasure of the Father in him. We have also seen that the Spirit led Jesus into the wilderness to test him and refine his character. Now we see that the Spirit also bestows particular purpose on Jesus. The Spirit anoints Jesus to take specific action (preaching good news to the poor, etc.) in a specific time and place (today, in your hearing).

How might Jesus have come to this conclusion? What enabled him to discern his calling? I think Luke gives us the necessary clues in his first four chapters. First, Luke shows us the faithfulness of Jesus' family context and the ways he was born and raised with a sense of calling. Though Jesus would not have had a specific memory of the manger and shepherds or Simeon and Anna, he heard the stories of God's faithfulness and the Spirit's work and how God had spoken to his mother and father about his destiny. Sometimes our family or community prepares us to discern the Spirit. Because of his family and history, Jesus was specifically listening and looking for the Spirit's lead.

Jesus' relationship with the Scriptures also shaped his general and specific sense of call. In chapter 2 Luke shows us that even at twelve years old Jesus had an appetite for the Word. He stayed behind in the temple in Jerusalem, learning and teaching with instructors of the Mosaic law. I wonder what he was learning about the Messiah during those extra days? When Jesus is tested by the devil in the wilderness, we see he had been reflecting on the text of Deuteronomy. And when he enters Nazareth, his word of calling comes directly from the prophecy of Isaiah. Jesus heard and understood the language of the Holy Spirit by soaking in the Scriptures.

Jesus' experience of the baptism and temptation also shaped his hearing of calling from God. At the baptism he experienced the Spirit in a powerful, physical descent like a bird. Luke says the Spirit descended on him "in bodily form like a dove" (Luke 3:22). This experience surely formed Jesus' expectancy of the Spirit's presence and movement. He also heard the voice of the Father confirming his primary calling as the beloved Son of the Father. He was able to rest in the pleasure of the Father—a pleasure that preceded any accomplishment of work. Then Jesus experienced the Spirit mysteriously leading him to the wilderness and into an extended fast. With the Spirit's help, he was able to respond faithfully to temptation and to clarify his identity and calling to worship only God. The Spirit gave him words from Deuteronomy to respond to each temptation. These experiences gave Jesus the foundation he needed in identity and character to discern the Spirit's leading him in "what to do."

We don't know exactly how Jesus understood his Isaiah 61 calling or his Nazareth moment. Those specifics remain mysterious. Luke does, however, repeat that the Spirit led him, called him, and empowered him. We also know some of the story. He was influenced by the voices of his family. He followed the pattern of the Scriptures. And he had sensory experiences of the Spirit's leadership. I take comfort in the fact that these are some of the same ways I discern the Spirit's movement in my life: through community and experience and especially Scripture.

DISCERNING OUR CALLING: SIGNPOSTS ON PILGRIMAGE

Jesus experienced the Spirit calling him. We can too. The Spirit shapes and leads us as disciples, forms us in character, and calls us to faith-filled, purposeful leadership in real time. But it's also complicated. Because of sin in and around us, our discernment of the Spirit's lead is imperfect at best. How then might we pay attention to the Spirit's calling on our lives?

Susi and I walked the Camino de Santiago—the Way of Saint James—across northern Spain in 2017. This 450-mile walk is known as a pilgrimage: a long journey of prayer. The Camino was a wonderful experience of prayer and healing for me, but my point here is that finding one's way on the Camino is a lot like discerning our calling with the help of the Holy Spirit.

When walking the Camino, the pilgrim must first establish the right general direction, toward Santiago from wherever the pilgrim is currently located. Sometimes it's not obvious, so we ask a local or another pilgrim, "Which way to Santiago?" and they point out the direction. Once on the path, you look for markers or signs pointing the correct direction. On the Camino, those markers generally take the design of a yellow arrow or scallop shell pointed in the direction toward Santiago (see figure 7.1). The scallop shell is a symbol of Saint James, who is said to have carried such a shell on his missionary journey, using it as a plate or bowl for food given to him. In his poverty James depended on the generosity of others and the guidance of the Spirit as he traveled.

As they walk, pilgrims need to pay close attention to signs in order not to miss a turn and get lost. This is most difficult in cities with their cacophony of noise and complexity. It is more difficult to see a small yellow arrow or shell when your senses are overwhelmed with input. As we walked through the larger cities of Bilbao, Santander, and Oviedo, we became anxious and had a difficult time finding our way. When we were unsure of our direction, we experienced a strong sense of dread. Walking ten to twenty miles a day for a month means you *really* don't want to get lost and walk extra. Sometimes when we would find a Camino marker, we would be so full of joy and relief that we would shout or cry a little.

In the end, our 450-mile walk was a series of thirty-four days of walking from one point to the next on our way

Figure 7.1. A marker along El Camino de Santiago

to Santiago. Each day was also a process of walking from one marker to the next, looking for signs of which way we should travel.

Our general direction is first. Christian discernment shares many qualities with navigating a pilgrimage. On the Camino, one needs to be headed toward Santiago rather than away from it. Left or right turns are irrelevant if you're going the wrong direction. So too with discerning our calling: first things are first. In the ministry of the Holy Spirit, God's priorities establish our larger direction. In this sense, the Spirit's highest values follow the outline of Luke 3 and 4. Repentance comes first, then baptism in the Father's love and pleasure, then character formation in the wilderness, and finally, out of all of those, discernment of "what to do." Sometimes we ask the Spirit about this or that job opportunity or relationship (or parking space!) but fail to ask first about our own repentance, intimacy with God, and character formation. When we do this, we get the order backward. We need to move in the right general direction, then look for signs of navigation.

In spiritual discernment, we begin with repentance. As far as we are able, we turn away from the idols in our lives and follow Jesus as Lord. Sometimes this makes certain decisions easy. My dad was an alcoholic who became a Christian and stopped drinking when I was very young. Back when he was drinking, he had been drawn to certain shady bars. When I was young, we always took very specific routes when driving around town. Later when I learned my own way around, I realized there were more efficient ways to get where we needed to go. I asked about this, and Dad told me he had decided never to drive by his former drinking haunts in order to remain faithful to Jesus. Sometimes our discernment is simple if we are committed to turning from idolatry and evil.

After repentance, we walk toward intimacy with God. At Jesus' baptism God the Father affirmed and blessed Jesus' identity ("my Son"), intimacy ("whom I love"), and pleasure ("with you I am well pleased"). The Holy Spirit will always affirm those same things in us. In considering a question of calling or discernment, we ask the Spirit how he wants to grow us in intimacy with him. It is important to prioritize this growth and stability. Sometimes this means prioritizing our mental and spiritual health over career or impact.

When I work with recent college graduates, I find they often want to know what they are supposed to do for a job, how to advance their career, or where they are supposed to live. They persevere in prayer, asking God for answers to these questions. But when they listen well to God, often they hear the Lord calling them first to a community and way of life. Often our church body, household, or family is the most important factor for our process of maturing in faith. We can expect that the Spirit will make our growth in faith a higher priority than our job or salary (though these also matter). When we set ourselves in the direction of growing in faith, we more readily see the Spirit's signposts regarding our next steps in the journey.

After intimacy, we consider character formation. The Spirit led Jesus into the wilderness for the hard "testing" work of formation. Because he loves us, he leads us in that direction as well. Sometimes we want the Spirit to speak to us about what to do, when the Spirit is more interested in who we are becoming. I have a good friend who recently left a high-level leadership position and thought the departure was about taking another (even higher) leadership position. That move did not work out, and my friend has been asking the Lord a lot of questions. He currently feels the Spirit leading him into a time of rest and healing—but he still needs an income. So he is looking for work but asking the Lord for something slower and more spacious. It takes courage to focus on how God is shaping our character. It is humbling. But when we turn ourselves in the direction of growing in character, we often find the Spirit giving us signs of calling.

Repentance, intimacy, and character are themes that get us headed in the right direction, toward Santiago. When we move that direction and look for the Spirit's signs, then we are more often able to find our way.

Of course, the fulfillment of God's kingdom is also our destination, and we move toward the values and purpose of his mission in the world. I have found, however, that pragmatically thinking of "mission" as our primary direction can sometimes cloud our discernment and compromise our integrity. For example, if missional effectiveness is our top priority, we may be tempted to compromise on sabbath keeping, prayer, or honesty about our struggles. God's mission is accomplished in paradoxical ways as his people choose to embody (rather than accomplish) his kingdom and grow in faith. If we are primarily pragmatic and strategic about mission, we often miss the mysterious work of the Spirit who begins with repentance, intimacy, and character in us. So we establish our direction based on receiving the love of Jesus and embodying his character—then we look for signs on our journey.

Our larger journey is made of smaller segments. Like on the Camino, in our calling we move in one general direction through many twists and turns on smaller segments. We look for signposts of the Spirit's direction and follow in his way. The brief stories of calling I shared at the beginning of this chapter (a particular word to be preached, a decision to move, and an encouragement to persevere) were a few of my encounters with signposts from the Spirit. In each of those experiences I received discernment for a specific step on the journey. That discernment mattered! Each one inspired a humble confidence that God was faithful and close and that I was seen and known. We all hunger for that confidence.

When you pass a signpost on the Camino, you are able to walk with greater freedom and less worry for the next section of road or trail. This is also true with discernment. When you have a sense, especially one confirmed in community, that you're following the Spirit's lead, you feel increased joy and freedom. On the Camino, each segment comes to an end and we must look for the next sign. So too in our journey of calling. Sometimes it feels easy to discern, and the signposts seem obvious and frequent. Other times we feel lost and alone, without a clear sense of the Spirit's direction. These seasons are what Saint John of the Cross referred to as a dark night of the soul, or a dark night of the senses, and they are actually common for believers.

While "dark night" can sound intense (and sometimes it *is* intense), all of us experience seasons of relative darkness in our lives. Many have short or long periods when God seems silent or we don't feel anything emotionally in connection with God. Others experience extended periods of confusion or doubt. When these "dark night" seasons come, it is crucial to continue seeking God in the ways we know and to continue looking for signs of the Spirit. It helps to go back and check on our main directional priorities. Do we need to repent of idolatry in any way? How might God deepen our intimacy with him? What does the Spirit want to do in forming our character? Sometimes this checkup will open our sense of God's leading. In these seasons it is also important to lean on community and trust the Scriptures. Community helps us move forward with faithfulness when we can't see for ourselves. The Scriptures also illuminate our path, even through a dark night.

In the experience of a dark night, the Lord is often inviting the believer to a deeper level of trust and a different kind of listening. Some of the contemplative saints of the past have been helpful to me in such seasons. Teresa of Ávila's sixteenth-century writings have helped me build on different kinds of prayer in different seasons of life. *Abandonment to Divine Providence* by Jean-Pierre de Caussade (1675–1751) has helped me learn to trust God's complete presence in moments when I don't sense it. Carlo Carretto's story has helped me learn to contemplate God's presence in my own experience of God's silence.

We look for signs of the Spirit's call every day, and we recognize that our journey may take unexpected turns when the Spirit gives us direction. Saint Ignatius of Loyola describes this lifestyle of discernment as "living with one foot raised." The image is of a disciple always ready to step forward out the door when the Spirit issues a call. I love this image of readiness or availability! The image of one foot raised reminds me to regularly ask whether the Spirit is calling me to make a significant change. I don't ask this every day, but periodically—either every few months or every few years.

There are times when I feel a sense of stability in the Spirit's call on me, and I am confident I'm in the right place and job with a good mix of rhythms and disciplines in my life. In those times I don't initiate a major discernment process. But when I'm internally stirred by persistent emotion or challenged by a particular Scripture, I stop and ask what the Spirit is doing and saying in my calling. Also, when I experience transition in job, family, or community, I often initiate a season of discernment in which I ask what the Spirit is doing. Sometimes the liturgical seasons of Advent or Lent lead me into discernment questions. In these times I find it helpful to clarify what questions I'm asking of the Lord and bring those questions to a group of friends who know me well. With the counsel of friends I decide what kind of discernment process is appropriate for my questions.

The segments combine to a pilgrimage. On the Camino de Santiago, a pilgrim walks one segment at a time. However, the pilgrim is always on a longer journey with a destination. As we walked toward Santiago, we talked with dozens of pilgrims. Each one had a unique story about why they were on the Camino and what they were seeking. Just as Santiago was the outer destination for all, each person also had an inner shape to their pilgrimage. We met a woman who had suffered many painful losses in her life and was walking to pray through her grief. Another woman was working through the pain of divorce and hoping to gain healing and strength. We met several young men and women in their twenties and thirties who had stepped out of successful careers because they realized they were unfulfilled. They were walking in pursuit of a new sense of meaning and purpose in their lives. This is the nature of pilgrimage—the journey has a distinct shape both outwardly on land and inwardly in the heart of the pilgrim.

This inward and outward nature is also true of Christian calling. As we discern God's invitation in our lives and as we follow his invitation step by step, we begin to discover the inner and outer shape of our call.

The outer shape of our call is analogous to a pilgrim's destination on land. It answers the question, *What does God intend to do with my life?* Sometimes it looks like career trajectory, but that can be deceiving because God's intentions are often not aligned with the human interests that shape careers. Please recognize that your job is not your calling, and your calling is not your job. Of course, the two are often related, and we want to pursue our calling in the context of our work. But calling is larger and more thematic.

As we follow the segments of God's leadership, we begin to see themes in terms of how God has gifted us and what God is consistently asking of us. Someone particularly gifted in data analysis may find that God consistently invites them to use that gift—and it becomes a pattern where that person recognizes God's consistent call. Of course, God may invite them to grow in areas of weakness as well. Sometimes a person discerns the outer shape of their calling by the passions of their heart. If a person is passionate for lost people to be saved, she may be called to evangelism. If he is passionate to feed the hungry, he may be called to mercy. Of course, we consider the passions of our heart in light of how God is also shaping our character.

The inner shape of our call is more aligned with meaning than purpose. While purpose is essentially practical and outwardly goal oriented, meaning is more abstract, philosophical, and personal. The inner shape of our call answers the question, *Who am I becoming?*

Let me give a couple of examples. Eugene Peterson is one of my heroes in ministry. Through many of his works Peterson clarifies that his outward calling was to be a pastor. In fact, he names his memoir *The Pastor.* Through many years and discernment periods, Peterson intentionally decided to stay in local pastoral ministry because of this call. Peterson's inner call, however, was to be a saint. Winn Collier's excellent recent biography of Peterson explores the passion that fueled Peterson's devotional life for many decades. He was working as a pastor but becoming a saint.

My wife, Susi, is a science fiction writer. She worked in direct ministry with InterVarsity for ten years but then recognized that her creative calling was to tell great stories. She does many things but gives much of her best energy to this outward calling as a writer. Inwardly, Susi has recognized over time that given her particular temperament, she grows best through deep theological reflection. This direction is not because she was initially drawn to theology. Rather, theological reflection has become a discipline for her. As she has pursued this discipline, she has found that God uses it to feed and mature her soul. She doesn't have a catchy slogan for it, but as I look at her inward call, I find that she is becoming a deeply thoughtful, prayerful soul. So as Susi looks for God's calling in her life step by step, she considers both her calling to write and also her deepening calling in prayer and reflection.

Our journey is indeed step by step, and the Spirit's invitation is sometimes surprising. Yet over time we recognize the shape of the journey both outwardly and inwardly. This recognized shape helps us look in the right places for signs of God's calling.

FINDING THE SIGNPOSTS

Let's get as practical as we can. On the Camino, a pilgrim learns how to look for yellow arrows or scallop shells pointing the way. So once we are set in the right general direction, where do we look for signposts of discernment on our journey? How does the Spirit reveal direction for God's people? I'm including an in-focus summary at the end of the chapter about how we listen well to discern the Spirit's lead. Here I will give a few encouragements specifically about calling.

First, we must simply pray. A lot. Prayer is where we will typically encounter signs from the Spirit about our calling. You may be charismatic or liturgical, Reformed or Anabaptist, Catholic or nondenominational. In any Christian tradition we can learn to see and hear the Spirit's calling if we pray. Even if you are not sure you believe in God at all, give prayer a try! I'm convinced that God especially loves to answer the prayers of skeptics. Sometimes we learn to pray by choosing what works for us. We join prayer meetings with others, are guided by devotionals, or follow liturgy. God speaks to us in what we like. Other times we learn prayer by choosing something that stretches us. I shared in earlier chapters how I learned from Orthodox iconography and the stations of the cross.

We also grow in prayer by finding someone who seems to know how to pray and asking that person for help. A mentor or spiritual director can help us grow in prayer. Prayer is by nature two-way communication with God, and we usually don't hear his voice unless we enter the conversation.

Second, we immerse ourselves in Scripture. Jesus found his responses to temptation in Deuteronomy 6–8. He found the calling expressed in Nazareth in Isaiah 61. The Holy Spirit's vocabulary for calling usually comes directly from Scripture, and it is always congruent with what's revealed in Scripture. Therefore, to the extent we are fluent with the Word we will be able to see and understand the signs of God's calling in our day-to-day life.

For me, this has meant focusing on certain sections of Scripture over certain periods of my life. The Gospels are always in my reading and study plan. They are key to understanding my faith and maintaining intimacy with Jesus. For the last fifteen years or so, I have also prayed through the Psalms each month in order to learn the Bible's themes of prayer. There have been times when I've majored on Old Testament Prophets or History, or New Testament Epistles. I want to know the Word because it helps me know God. The Word also helps me interpret the Spirit's lead in my life. Often the Spirit seems to highlight a particular Scripture as relevant for a period of my life. That focus will last for a week or a month or a year, and as I pray through that passage, it often becomes the signpost telling me what to do in a situation. Right now I'm finding Psalm 16 to be that passage, and it is shaping the way I engage each day.

Third, we engage with community. Following Jesus is a communal activity with individual elements—not the other way around. The body of Christ in the world is communal, and most of the commands and invitations in Scripture are addressed to communities (the *you* is usually plural). So when looking for signs of the Spirit's call, we should look together and receive help from those around us. The most discerning communities include a diverse set of perspectives and cultures.

I have been part of a covenant group of five men for over twenty-five years now. We started meeting together in our thirties in order to hold each other accountable in areas of faith, family, and ministry. Whenever any of us have questions of calling, we process and discern together. If my life is in question or crisis, I often find that the four other men in the group see me more clearly than I see myself.

Fourth, we grow in self-awareness. Knowledge of ourselves is key to awareness of how God may be calling us. Assessments of spiritual gifts or temperament can help us on the journey of self-understanding. It is better not to focus on just one category or assessment but to take many into account. It's also helpful to engage community in order to understand ourselves. When we see ourselves with increasing clarity, we can begin to identify when our desires are invitations from God and when they are temptations. Eventually as we know ourselves and listen to the Spirit, we find that our calling has a general shape and trajectory.

By my late thirties, I recognized repeated themes in my call. I saw themes of priest, prophet, and missionary in my vocation. The Spirit seemed to consistently invite me in those three directions. In my case, those three images spoke to both my outer calling (what I do) and my inner calling (who I am becoming). In my fifties, I saw the Spirit more specifically inviting me to a priestly leadership, which I understood to be leadership that is fundamentally prayerful and pastoral. The clarification of basic shape has helped me look specifically for how the Spirit may invite me next. I don't presume the Spirit will call me in a certain direction, but like a pilgrim on the Camino, I look for the signs where they are most likely to be posted.

Fifth, we look at our context. From the ministry of John in the wilderness, we have practiced looking at the topography of our social context in order to understand how the Word arrives and calls us to the good news of repentance. Sometimes the needs and opportunities presented by our context or moment in history become signposts of our calling. Let me clarify that I don't think need equates with calling. There will always be needs we are not called to meet. Until Jesus returns, our world will continue to be broken and hurting, and we are not responsible for all of that brokenness and hurt. But Jesus does have compassion for every hurt and need, and often he calls his people to minister to those needs.

Oscar Romero was a parish priest in El Salvador in the 1970s. He was a faithful, vibrant minister in his local community and was extremely devoted to Scripture and prayer. In 1977 during a season of national crisis when thousands of poor people were being oppressed and killed, Father Romero was appointed archbishop over the church in El Salvador. From that position, Romero recognized a new call from the Holy Spirit to specifically be the pastor and the voice of the poor across his country. His call had not previously been to engage government or cry for justice, but the Spirit used a moment in history to clarify his vocation for that last season of his life. As we look for signs of the Spirit's call, we must also look around us at context and history, recognizing that the Spirit speaks into particular dynamics at particular times.

Finally, we often find the shape of our calling by looking at our conversion story. I am indebted to Gordon T. Smith for his research and insights about this specific pattern. I attended a seminary class taught by Dr. Smith in which the group (all InterVarsity staff) reflected and wrote extended narratives of how we came to faith. Then we reflected on how God was working in our lives and calling since that time. Every single one of us found significant resonance between the themes of our conversion and the themes of how God has called us since that time. The Spirit seems to call people in similar ways from the beginning to the end of their Christian journeys.

We often hunger to know our calling at certain moments or stages of life. We want, like Jesus, to be able to say, "Today this Scripture is fulfilled in your hearing." I believe we can actually discern God's calling day by day and year by year in our lives, but it is messy work. Because we are messy people, we start by looking at our overall direction in the form of repentance, intimacy, and character formation. Then we can look for signs of God's calling. The more we say yes to those signs, the more we will want to continue following them.

PRACTICE: PRAY WITH ISAIAH 61

In this exercise I invite you into an imaginative prayer journey with the beginning of Isaiah 61.

Begin by thinking about the social circles and situations in your life. Who are the people and institutions closest to you? Who are those one or two levels out? Where are there resources and lack of resources among those people and institutions? It may be helpful to draw a diagram or list them out. When you've sketched out your social world, spend a few minutes offering the people and institutions and dynamics to God.

Set your imagination for the reading of Isaiah 61 this way. Imagine Jesus, coming into your community, filled with the power of the Holy Spirit. Imagine him gathering your whole social world, as represented by the list or diagram you made. And then imagine him coming and speaking the words of Isaiah 61:1-3:

> The Spirit of the Sovereign LORD is on me,
>> because the LORD has anointed me
>> to proclaim good news to the poor.
>
> He has sent me to bind up the brokenhearted,
>> to proclaim freedom for the captives
>> and release from darkness for the prisoners,
> to proclaim the year of the LORD's favor
>> and the day of vengeance of our God,
> to comfort all who mourn,
>> and provide for those who grieve in Zion—
> to bestow on them a crown of beauty
>> instead of ashes,

the oil of joy
   instead of mourning,
and a garment of praise
   instead of a spirit of despair.
They will be called oaks of righteousness,
   a planting of the LORD
   for the display of his splendor.

- Spend some moments taking note of what you experienced or imagined as Jesus spoke those words of Isaiah to your community.
- In what ways does Jesus want to speak good news to the poor in your world?
- In what ways might he bind up the brokenhearted?
- What prisoners or dynamics of captivity exist in your world? How might Jesus want to liberate them?
- What would the year of the Lord's favor and the day of God's vengeance look like in your world?
- How might Jesus want to comfort those who mourn?
- Imagine the oaks of righteousness God wants to raise up and pray for them.

Considering all these questions, offer your prayers to God. Ask the Holy Spirit to speak to you, and pay attention to how the Spirit might send you as an answer to your prayers.

SPIRIT, WORD, AND COMMUNITY

THE HOLY SPIRIT SHAPES US as disciples and calls us as leaders—but how does that work? Jesus did a great job of following the lead of the Spirit, but we often struggle to even notice the Spirit. How might we better perceive and cooperate with the Spirit's work? This summary may help us understand the fundamentals of discerning the Spirit's presence and movement.

Listen for the Spirit as embodied creatures. The Holy Spirit lives within us and leads us through all of our senses. We attend to him by paying attention to our bodies and our emotions, our mind and our senses. The Spirit can lead us through experiences, ideas, words, images, or feelings. Of course, not all of our senses and feelings are from the Spirit—but we start by paying attention to our whole being.

Look for the themes of the Spirit's movement. The Holy Spirit has several key roles, according to Scripture. When we tune our attention to those areas, we are better able to notice his presence and movement.

- The Spirit testifies to God's love. I believe this is the Spirit's most fundamental role. We begin to listen to the Spirit by praying for a sense of God's love for us (Galatians 4:6-7; Romans 8:15).

- The Spirit leads us into the ways and words of Jesus. Since the Holy Spirit is one in personhood with Jesus, he will always witness to the words of Jesus and follow the methods of Jesus (John 14:25-27).

- The Spirit convicts us of sin and leads us in righteousness (John 16:8). Though the Spirit does not shame us, he often reveals where we need to repent in order to embrace his kingdom.

Discern the Spirit's work in community. Just as the church is only communally the body of Christ (no individual but Jesus can claim that), so also the Holy Spirit is given communally to God's people. Since we receive the Spirit as a community, it is best to discern the Spirit's work communally. Our sisters and brothers help us perceive the move of the Spirit.

Measure by the standard of Scripture. The Spirit's work will always be congruent with the Scriptures. To the extent that we read, meditate on, and study the Scriptures, we will be more able to sense the Spirit's leading.

I don't always feel the same feelings or see the Spirit lead in the same way. But I do test the experiences I'm having, in order to see if they are the Spirit leading. I test them first through their congruence with God's revelation in Scripture and the typical roles of the Spirit. Then I test whether the experience is in line with the fruit of God's Spirit and God's call on my life. Finally I test them in community with others. Over time this process has become more natural and organic for me, and I've gained greater fluency in sensing the Spirit's movement. But I always need to test my experiences in the above ways.

8

CYCLES OF DISCERNMENT

Following the Roundabout Way

Lord, teach us to discern your presence and leadership through the stages and cycles of our lives. We want to grow close to you, and we also want to participate in your kingdom purposes. We are often confused and disoriented. We need you to open our senses to your leading so we might cooperate with your Spirit and trust you.

In an American dream paradigm, the graph of formation and leadership follows a line up and to the right, where our maturity and sphere of influence only keep increasing. I have seen a lot of young leaders stumble because of this linear assumption, in two ways. One group of leaders assumes that God's favor will always be shown in an increase toward the next challenge, the next level of responsibility, and the next level of comfort and privilege. Then when they experience something different (for example, a significant failure at work), they become discouraged, depressed, or angry toward God.

Another group assumes that God has assigned them to always increase in leadership. After a few promotions or successes, they consistently push for more authority and choose to go forward with it. In due time, these leaders' authority exceeds their character and they crash in moral or emotional failure.

God's ways often don't match our linear assumptions. If you read the stories of the saints, you find that comfort, wealth, and success do not always increase over time. In experience, the Lord leads his faithful people in progress toward his kingdom purposes, but then seemingly toward failure and desperation, and later to more progress. We experience loss, victory, disorientation, comfort, and desolation. Sometimes the changes are so extreme it feels like whiplash in our souls.

I experienced this whiplash between 2015 and 2017. From 2011 to 2015 things had been going well for me. I was growing in my faith and stretched in my calling. I worked as hard as I ever had and was experiencing focus and affirmation in my work. But in 2016 I encountered heartbreaking organizational challenges and conflicts. In those conflicts I lost many friendships I held dear. I carried substantial responsibility in facing the challenges, and I felt conflicting feelings. On one side I felt I had been as faithful as I could be. On the other side I experienced a sense of profound failure. I wondered how God could have led me (and us as an organization) on such a path.

In the midst of that challenging season, we had a major organizational restructuring. In that process I was invited by others to apply for a challenging job. I felt the Lord's invitation to follow through. I applied faithfully and was confused when I was not selected. Again, I asked the Lord why he had led me on this confusing way. Two great encouragements followed for me in 2017. The first was a sabbatical period when I was able to receive some deep healing from the wounds of conflict, challenge, and rejection. With healing I also gained greater clarity about what God was doing in me and through me. Second, after the restructure, I had the opportunity to help create a position, apply for that job, and be hired for it. The challenges, conflicts, rejection, and healing I experienced from 2015 to early 2017 allowed me to create and fill the position in which I'm still serving now.

THE ROUNDABOUT WAY

The people of God experienced this whiplash as they followed the pillar of cloud and fire through the wilderness. As he recorded their experience, Moses called it "the roundabout way":

So God led the people by the roundabout way of the wilderness toward the Red Sea. (Exodus 13:18 NRSVCE)

Remember how the LORD your God led you all the way in the wilderness these forty years, to humble and test you in order to know what was in your heart, whether or not you would keep his commands. (Deuteronomy 8:2)

As leaders, we usually prefer the direct route. We like to achieve results as efficiently as possible. When God delivered the Israelites from slavery, he took them to the wilderness for worship. From the wilderness, they likely expected that God would lead them directly toward the Promised Land. However, the Lord led them the roundabout way toward the Red Sea and later through forty years of wilderness wandering. The turn toward the Red Sea brought the people of God into a true crisis, as the Egyptian army bore down on them with murderous rage. The people were trapped and vulnerable. There was no path of escape. They depended on the Lord for a miracle, and he delivered them across the sea and killed their enemies. This resulted in a quintessential moment of worship on the far shore, where Moses and Miriam led the people in singing to the Lord (see Exodus 15:1-21). God fulfilled their going into the wilderness to worship, but he did it in a more difficult way than they imagined.

Deuteronomy tells us that the long, forty-year winding path through the wilderness was for God's people to learn to trust God's words and provision (see Deuteronomy 8:2-5). In the wilderness God taught them again and again to trust and follow him. Though it was difficult for the people to understand, God was doing a deep work of formation in them. In some ways it was like a honeymoon for the Israelites to become more intimate with God. Thomas Merton describes it this way:

The Desert Fathers believed that the wilderness had been created as supremely valuable in the eyes of God precisely because it had no value to men. The wasteland was the land that could never be

wasted by men because it offered them nothing. There was
nothing to attract them. There was nothing to exploit. The desert
was the region in which God's Chosen People had wandered for
forty years, cared for by God alone. They could have reached the
Promised Land in a few months if they had traveled directly.
God's plan was that they should learn to love Him in the wilderness and that they should always look back on the time in the
desert as the idyllic time of their life with Him alone.

God leads in roundabout ways we don't understand, because God sees
something better for us. His purposes within and among us are as
important to God as his purposes in transforming the world. How, as
leaders and disciples, can we best discern his paradoxical leading?

FINDING A PATTERN

It helps to pull the camera back for a wide-angle perspective on God's
direction. Here's how I understand our labyrinthine, roundabout path
from a theological perspective. God is the protagonist of history, and
we are supporting characters in God's story. We as his disciples and as
leaders participate in God's plans as we learn to follow the Holy Spirit.
As we follow the Spirit, we begin to experience God's roundabout
ways, because God's thoughts are higher than our understanding. We
must first admit our frustration that God takes us on ways we do not
choose. Then we can learn to believe in God's good intentions and
trust that he is doing what he does both for our own good and for his
ultimate purposes.

As Christian leaders, if we can discern the work of the Spirit in our
lives, we will be more able to cooperate with the Spirit's leadership in
the world. Therefore we look for patterns that help us diagnose the
Spirit's movement and leadership. We discover those patterns through
Scripture and as we practice saying yes to the Spirit's invitations. In the
rest of this chapter, I'll offer two patterns that can help us diagnose the
Spirit's direction. After that, I will invite you into some practices that
sharpen discernment.

PATTERN ONE: THE CYCLE FROM LUKE 3–4

In Luke, Jesus goes through a certain process as the Spirit leads him. He arrives in the wilderness where the word has come to John. He progresses to baptism in the Jordan where he receives the anointing of the Spirit and the Father's words of identity, affection, and pleasure. Luke notes Jesus' genealogy next, evoking the blessings and challenges of family and culture. Jesus follows the Spirit's lead back into the wilderness, where he is tested and formed in character. He then returns to Nazareth in the power of the Spirit, having discerned his Isaiah 61 calling. In Nazareth he directly engages the fulfillment of his calling. Even as Jesus proclaims the fulfillment of his calling, he experiences opposition as the crowd in Nazareth tries to murder him. So the Spirit has led Jesus from wilderness to baptism to temptation to calling and action—and on to resistance. For Christian leaders, I see this as a cycle that repeats again and again. The roundabout way for us looks like what we see in figure 8.1.

Figure 8.1. The Luke 3–4 leadership cycle

I'm not suggesting that this cycle is a precise formula. The stages often go in order, but sometimes they skip around. The different

elements serve better as a diagnostic than a strategy: they help us recognize how the Lord is working in our formation and leadership. Most
often, after a fruitful "Nazareth" season, the Lord has led me into a
wilderness season of repentance or waiting—but sometimes I go directly to character formation. The pattern doesn't tell me what to do,
but it helps me discern what God is doing in my journey and pay attention to the Spirit's leadership.

In my late twenties I went through an intense period where I moved
all the way around the cycle: from Nazareth to wilderness to baptism
to genealogy to temptation. Initially I was leading more effectively
than I had ever experienced. I felt a strong sense of the Spirit's empowerment and calling in my work with students, and the work itself was
flourishing. I felt like I was in Nazareth fulfilling my calling in real time.

But then a dramatic set of conflicts in my team and among students
sent me into the deepest sense of failure and depression I had ever
experienced. In my desolation, I sought the Lord and tried to listen for
his word. Honestly, it was difficult for me to sense any movement from
the Spirit at that time. The word was not "working" for me in the way
I expected. I was literally asking God, my supervisor, Susi, and my
friends the same questions people asked John in the wilderness: "What
then shall I do?" I was in the wilderness of John, waiting for the word
of the Lord.

I distinctly remember the day I realized at least one answer to my
question—I should get some therapy. It felt like a new revelation to me,
but Susi and my friends had actually been saying it for a while. In
therapy I experienced the baptism and genealogy stages with vibrancy.
I explored the family systems that made me so afraid of failure and
conflict. My counselor helped me connect with the affection and
pleasure of God apart from my performance. Though I felt emotionally
desolate, I found God loving me and healing me.

My counselor gave me assignments to pursue particular kinds of
conversations with my family and my staff team. The Spirit used those
assignments to lead me through a temptations phase. I remember a

conversation with my mother that felt like jumping off a cliff. As instructed by my therapist, I had a conversation with Mom that broke from the scripts and expectations that had defined my whole life. Mom's feelings and their impact on me had been off-limits in the culture of my family. It sounds silly, but I could not conceive of talking with Mom about her emotions or the way they affected me. Feedback like that was out of bounds. The only way (at least in my own mind) to address her feelings was through performance. If I performed well, she would be happy.

I was terrified, but I took the risk to directly address how I had been impacted by her emotions and how I was now changing. It was difficult to do, but Mom responded quite well. God used that conversation and many others to reshape my character and teach me new ways to live. Those risks of faith broke some of the power that evil held in my life, and they released me to follow the Spirit's lead more freely.

In the kingdom of God, our pathway is not up and to the right. Rather, it looks more like a spiral. We keep going around the stages, but always in different ways. By God's mercy we move deeper in healing, formation, and calling. After that transformative period of therapy in my midtwenties, I "graduated" with a clean bill of health. But my pathway of growth and leadership has led me back to healing and character formation several more times since then.

A few years ago in my midfifties I again discerned the Spirit's invitation into therapy. I was regularly experiencing anxiety in certain relationships, and I was also consistently feeling a pain in my chest. I remember the hopeful realization that what I kept feeling in my chest was probably trauma, and I could get some help with that! In therapy God led me again to experience the baptism dynamic of God meeting me with love and pleasure in my most painful moments. I again felt healed and also challenged to grow in character. I again finished a season of counseling.

I don't know if I'll go back to therapy, but I'm confident the Spirit will continue to lead me through cycles of repentance, healing, and formation as well as calling and fruitfulness. I find the paradigm of wilderness, baptism, genealogy, temptation, and Nazareth helpful as a diagnostic tool. I regularly ask the Holy Spirit in prayer, "Where am I now in this cycle?" I also ask that question of my family and friends, who sometimes see the Spirit's work in my life more clearly than I do.

The cyclical, spiral shape of formation describes the Spirit's work better than the linear graph of growth. When we look for the Spirit's leadership with the spiral in mind, we are more likely to perceive his movement.

PATTERN TWO: SEASONS

Scripture gives us another diagnostic framework for the roundabout way of our formation and calling: the seasonality of a fruit-bearing tree. This pattern does not necessarily correspond to the last one—they are both simply diagnostics that help us get a sense of God's presence and movement in our lives.

Psalm 1 speaks of the one who meditates on God's Word as a tree planted by waters, bearing its fruit in season. Jesus speaks of the vine and branches in John 15. And in Jeremiah 17:7-8, the Lord says:

> Blessed is the one who trusts in the LORD,
>   whose confidence is in him.
> They will be like a tree planted by the water
>   that sends out its roots by the stream.
> It does not fear when heat comes;
>   its leaves are always green.
> It has no worries in a year of drought
>   and never fails to bear fruit.

It helps me to think of what happens to a tree in different seasons and what that might mean in our formation as disciples and leaders. The organic metaphor of seasons also helps us recognize the roundabout way. Our growth and calling are not always up and to the right—we experience pruning and barrenness as well as increase and fruit.

Of course, a leader's growth is seldom an annual cycle—some seasons of the soul last just a few weeks, while others last for years. If we can identify the season we are experiencing, though, we can embrace the important growth that's happening and prepare well for the season that will likely follow.

In the fall, the energy-producing chlorophyll in leaves stops being produced, and life-giving sugars and nutrients travel down to the roots of the tree. As the chlorophyll drains from the leaves, they lose their green color and return to their natural yellow or red pigment. Also in the fall, farmers prune trees back in ways that often look severe. Branches are trimmed and cut in order to prepare for maximum fruit bearing the following summer. For Christian leaders, the fall season can be one of reflection, pruning, and repentance. This is challenging, especially for leaders who assume that productivity should always increase! Rather than assuming perpetual growth, we can look at the fruit and life of the past season and ask the Spirit what to cut back and how to focus our thoughts and energy. Like we do in the wilderness of John the Baptist, we wait for the word of the Lord and repent of our idolatries.

In the winter, trees store their energy underground in the roots. A deciduous tree looks barren during these cold months, but it remains alive and well below the surface. For Christians, a winter season may involve challenging feelings of barrenness, cold, and darkness. These seasons are often when God leads us to formation at the level of our being. God wants to heal and strengthen the roots of our family or cultural narratives and wounds. As in the baptism of Jesus, he wants to assure us of the identity, affection, and pleasure only he can give. Also as in the baptism, the Spirit's work in a winter season seems separate from outward, productive work.

In spring, trees awaken from slumber and bring their vibrancy forward in buds, blossoms, and leaves. Spring is a season of mystery, where the character and shape of the year's harvest are revealed. Spring looks and smells of possibilities. For the soul of a Christian leader, a spring season is also full of mystery and potential. We begin to perceive the shape and the aroma of future harvest. It is a season of becoming and can be associated with character formation. We are often tempted to focus a spring season on outward productivity, but this would be premature. The mysteries of our becoming are often full of temptation for us, as Jesus experienced when the Spirit led him to the wilderness. In springtime periods, we pay attention to the testing and shaping of our character as well as the hope of what God may be promising.

Summer is the season of fruit bearing and harvest. This is when the tree spends nearly all its energy in production of fruit. The look and smell of ripeness dominates the orchard or vineyard, such that the birds are fed with overflowing abundance. For Christian leaders, these summer seasons are like Jesus' entry into Nazareth, where he experiences the Lord fulfilling the Scripture in real time. Summer is the season of intensive work to fulfill our calling, to produce the culture and influence God has invited from us. It often feels like joyful exhaustion and gratitude for God's fruit-producing grace.

As I write today, I'm experiencing a winter season of my soul. I described it in the last chapter as depletion. It feels a bit mysterious, honestly. I'm not positive where I'm at in the Luke 3–4 pattern (probably testing), but the winter season strikes me as an apt description of my experience. My inner life for the last year or more has felt cold and bare. I'm more tired and weak than usual. Though I am healthy, my capacity is diminished. I feel alive at the root level of my life: prayer is consistently engaging, Scripture is nourishing, and my relationships are loving and deep. In the most fundamental ways, I'm well. And yet I have experienced much death and grief in my close community. These winterish feelings are leading me to look for the Spirit's work under the surface of my outer work. I find that the Lord is working on my character these days, addressing my temptation to find identity in strength and energy. I'm asking the Holy Spirit how he might want to strengthen my roots in preparation for spring growth.

Perhaps the metaphor of seasons resonates more with you than the spiral of themes from Luke 3–4. If that's the case, ask God to give you more insight into what he is doing in your journey of growth and fruitfulness! The Spirit's movement in nature is a faithful reflection of how he also works in our souls and can help us cooperate with his formation.

DISCERNMENT SKILLS FROM SAINT IGNATIUS

The patterns above give us something of a map to help find where we are (and where we may be going) on the roundabout way. With a map we can find ourselves in the wilderness, at the Jordan, or entering Nazareth. We can find ourselves in a particular season of growth. In order to read well and navigate toward our destination, we need practical skills in reading both the map and the landscape around us. The historic Christian word for those navigational skills is *discernment*.

How do we follow this winding path? How do we discern the Spirit's lead when he surprises us on a roundabout way? We pray and listen, asking the Holy Spirit to reveal what he's doing and lead us in next steps. We take stock of the major temptations of fear on one side and pride on the other—and we walk the narrow path of tender humility combined with bold faith. We feed on the Scriptures, looking for guidance. We read our social context, looking for the Spirit's word and work in our community. As we read our context, we follow God's lead and pay special attention to the marginalized. We ask our community for feedback. We check the basic direction on our pilgrimage, then look for signs along the way. Finally, we look at patterns like we find in Luke 3–4 or in the seasons of a tree. Those patterns help us diagnose what is happening in our soul and cooperate with the Spirit's work.

In addition, we can learn from the wisdom of Saint Ignatius of Loyola, the founder of the Jesuit order. One of the great strengths of Ignatian spirituality is its focus on spiritual discernment. I offer a basic and practical guide here and more resources in the notes.

A posture of discernment: engaged indifference. Ignatius describes the ideal posture to discern God's work as indifference. In a posture of indifference, we acknowledge and then let go of all that demands our attention or allegiance, surrendering those attachments to the leadership of Jesus. Our indifference is not apathy. In order to surrender our attachments to Jesus, we actually need to be engaged with God and our context enough to recognize those attachments. I find it helpful to name the posture "engaged indifference" because it emphasizes how intentional we must be in surrendering to God's leadership. Stephen Macchia labels this posture "practicing a preference for God." I love the way Macchia's expression captures the nature of engaged indifference. We care about all that is going on and how it affects us and others—yet we surrender all of it to God as we consider the question of discernment.

Another preliminary practice in any discernment process is shaping a clear question that we are asking God. A clear question allows us to identify our related attachments and specifically surrender them to God. When we come to God with a clear question and a posture of engaged indifference, we are ready to discern the Spirit's leadership.

Two poles of discernment: consolation and desolation. Ignatius offers us a helpful polarity that clarifies our discernment. On one side we find consolation, which refers to the experience or state of deep connection with God. Consolation is not the same as happiness or contentment or comfort—it is a state of relationship with God. We experience consolation when we recognize the grace of God at work in and around us. We can know consolation in the midst of suffering and grief or in a time of celebration. Consolation involves both experience and recognition.

On the other side of the polarity we identify desolation, which refers to an experience or state of disconnection with God. As with consolation, desolation is not an emotional state of sadness or pain. Rather, it is the experience of disconnection with God's grace and presence. In desolation we are unable or unwilling to recognize God's love and leading.

For Ignatius, this polarity becomes a helpful tool of discernment. As we consider a discernment question, Ignatius teaches us to reflect and identify our experiences of consolation and desolation. In

Macchia's words, we then practice a preference for God by leaning toward consolation. Our highest goal is to cooperate with God's purposes and movement in us and in the world, so we steer our lives toward consolation. We almost always live with a mix of consolation and desolation in our lives, so steering toward consolation is a great rule of thumb for discernment.

Here's a practical example of how I help others use consolation and desolation in a group discernment process. First we work on clarifying the discernment question, to the point that it can be written down as one concise question. I will write that question on a flip chart and place it before us. Then I'll set up two more flip chart sheets—one labeled "Consolation" and the other labeled "Desolation." On the consolation sheet we write every experience related to the question that has in the past increased a sense of intimacy with God. On the desolation sheet we write every experience that has decreased intimacy with God. Then we come back to the question and ask if anything has become clearer.

Ignatius also gives a helpful warning: he tells us not to make any major decisions in a state of desolation. By "a state of desolation" he means a pervasive state of disconnection with God. In this situation, when a believer feels far from God and does not recognize God's leadership, Ignatius says it is better to delay all major decisions until a state of consolation can be found. Our first job in a state of pervasive desolation is to seek God, not to seek God's direction—and usually we do well to ask for help from others in this state. I have found this advice helpful in my own journey and as I have counseled others.

Discernment's core practice: examen. Ignatius then gives us a very practical path. He calls it the daily examination of conscience, but the Jesuits have typically shortened it to the examen. In this practice we spend a few minutes every day reflecting on our experiences of consolation and desolation and identifying how the Spirit may be leading us. The examen happens in three simple stages. Many have made translations of these stages, but my personal formulation is to ask these three questions:

- *Consolation.* Where have you sensed God's presence today? Take note and give thanks.

- *Desolation.* Where have you missed or betrayed his presence? Take note and ask forgiveness.

- *Discernment.* What one request or question are you holding before him in this season of life? Ask and wait.

I usually do my daily examen in the chair in my bedroom before sleep. I journal for a few minutes, bringing to mind the experience of my day and answering these three questions. Often, a memory surprises me as either a consolation or a desolation. I recognize God's active grace in a place that felt hard or see my own sin where I didn't before. Mostly, I recognize a lot more grace than I noted during the day, and my heart becomes more peaceful and grateful. Over time this practice has helped me be more attentive to the Spirit's movement in real time and more able to discern God's leading along my path.

When we practice the examen as a daily discernment tool, we become more able to discern the Spirit's leading in major decisions.

AN INTENTIONAL DISCERNMENT PROCESS

In times of major decision, it can be helpful to set up a formal discernment process. In 2017, Susi and I needed to decide whether to move across the country from Berkeley, California, to Madison, Wisconsin. As I have already described, I experienced the roundabout way quite severely from 2015 to early 2017. I was surprised by crisis and conflict and loss, by an opportunity and a closed door, by the grace of healing, and by another open door. With my new job, I was strongly encouraged (but not required) to move to Madison and serve from InterVarsity's national office.

Susi and I were tense. The stakes were high in considering a move. We had lived in Berkeley for twenty-nine years and raised our children there. Our kids, Abby and Gabe, now adults, both lived in California and were inclined to stay. On the other hand, the invitation to move and start new seemed like a promising opportunity, especially for my work. So we initiated an intentional discernment process. We gathered a group of core friends who knew us well and reserved three dates to meet together over the course of a few months. These were amazing friends, fully surrendered to God and willing to pray and discern with us.

In the first meeting we prayed together, shaped our discernment question, talked about the process, and prayed some more. Each time we prayed with the group, we went around and asked each person to share any impressions or Scriptures they had heard in prayer. In shaping the question, we started with the obvious: "Should we move to Madison?" By God's grace, the question expanded to, "Should we move to Madison? Why or why not?" In any discernment process, the question is important and *why* questions are often helpful to consider. At this point our decision was full of tension. It felt like a move to Madison would be a win for me and a great loss for Susi. The whole group felt the tension and prayed for God's leading.

In the second meeting, we again prayed and checked in at the beginning and end of the time. We adapted a couple of practical exercises from Ignatius and applied them to our discernment question. One was a simple listing of costs and benefits of each path. Another was a prayer experience where we "tried on" each decision and looked for the signs of the Holy Spirit and signs of the spirit of temptation. Both of these exercises began to turn the group's perspective toward the state of our marriage and what God might be doing in our relationship. We ended that time focused more on the *why* part of the question than the *whether to move* part.

Between the second and third group meeting, Susi and I both felt the Spirit move us to focus on what God was calling for in our relationship for the next season of life. We recognized that the move was an invitation for us to live our life and calling more together and less separately. Through discernment, our decision became less of a win-lose decision. God was leading us toward shared opportunity rather than compromise. By the time of our third meeting, we believed that God was calling us to move. We gathered the group to listen to the Lord and give either confirmation or challenge to our decision. Through prayer and conversation, the whole group confirmed the sense of God's leading. Our adult daughter, Abby, was living with us in Berkeley at the time, and Gabe was in San Diego. Our decision to move and sell our home was costly for Abby (who had to move out), but she was also convinced of God's leading and supportive of our move.

We have now been in Wisconsin for over five years, and one of my greatest joys is in the shared life of our marriage. God has been fulfilling his invitation for our relationship to flourish and bear fruit in shared hospitality and ministry.

PRACTICE: WALK A LABYRINTH

The labyrinth is an embodied prayer practice that helps us process the roundabout way. Christian labyrinths date back to an Algerian basilica in 324 CE. When we walk and pray through a labyrinth, our bodies experience the twists and turns of a roundabout path (see figure 8.2).

Figure 8.2. A labyrinth

Start by finding a labyrinth near you. Try www.labyrinthlocator .com or a simple Google search. Prepare by spending some time in discernment, asking the Spirit what he wants you to pray about. Carry an intention—a specific prayer or struggle you are experiencing. If helpful, carry a stone or another symbol to represent your intention. Pray for guidance.

Walk through the labyrinth slowly and listen for the Spirit. Note any Scriptures that come to mind.

- On the way in, surrender your will to the Lord and ask for freedom and trust. Listen for his word.

- In the center, pause to receive from God. Listen awhile. Note any impressions the Lord puts on your heart. Leave your stone or symbol at the center of the labyrinth, offering it to God.

- On the way out, integrate what you have received from God. Give thanks for God's presence on the roundabout way. Worship.

After coming out, journal any words or symbols that the Lord gave you and give thanks for his guidance.

GROUP GUIDE 5

BIBLE STUDY: LUKE 4:14-30 (25 MINUTES)

Read Luke 4:14-22 aloud.

- Describe the dynamic in verses 14-15. What was the tone? What might the article headlines have been if such things existed at the time?

- Describe the scene at the synagogue in Nazareth.

- Why do you think Jesus chose this particular passage in Isaiah (Isaiah 61:1-2)?

- Describe the group's response so far.

Read Luke 4:23-30 aloud.

- Paraphrase what you think Jesus was trying to say in verses 23-27.

- Why do you think Jesus provoked them in this way?

- Why do you think they responded so strongly?

- If you are able, tell a story of when you heard something that initially seemed wonderful and affirming but later felt challenging or offensive.

- If Jesus came to your group today, what do you think his message would be?

GROUP DISCUSSION QUESTIONS FOR
CHAPTERS 7–8 (35 MINUTES)

Discerning calling

1. If you're able, describe one experience where you felt called by God.

2. Give your best attempt at describing God's calling for your group or team.

3. In the Camino metaphor, describe an experience of finding the right general direction in your own life or for your group.

4. Describe a discernment experience of looking for a specific signpost. How did you (or how would you like to) get clear discernment in that situation?

5. Describe what the inner (becoming) calling might be for your group. What might the outer (doing) calling be?

6. In light of the In Focus resource on Spirit, Word, and Community, what are your (and your group's) strengths and weaknesses in discerning the Spirit?

The roundabout way

7. How have you experienced the "roundabout way" dynamic of surprise or whiplash?

8. Which pattern (stages of Luke 3–4 or seasons of the soul) resonated most with you? Share where you think you are at in that pattern.

9. Where might your group or team be in the Luke pattern or the seasons pattern?

10. Which of the Ignatian discernment practices seemed most relevant to you?

11. How might your group or team adopt a discernment practice?

PRAYER AS LEADERSHIP

From Action to Dependence

Lord Jesus, teach us to pray. Let our discipleship growth and our leadership influence flow out of conversation with you. Shape us to become like you in every way. Call us, Lord, to join you as you mediate the purposes of heaven in the gritty realities of our lives. And in the end, glorify yourself through our worship as your kingdom and will are established on earth.

As should be clear by now, I'm a fan of Ignatius of Loyola, the founder of the Society of Jesus (the Jesuits). I've learned and grown through studying Jesuit history and theology and by experiencing their spiritual exercises formation program. However, one thing has bugged me for a long time about the Jesuits. Their motto is "Toward the greater glory of God." They include it on many of their publications with the initials for the motto in Latin: AMDG+. What bugs me is this: how can we ever increase God's glory? Isn't God's glory in the hands of God alone? It seems like a lot of pressure and possibly presumption.

But on a recent prayer retreat I came to understand that there's another way to think about it. I realized I needed to stop thinking about our participation in the greater glory of God like an engine and instead think of it like an antenna. If our leadership is an engine driving the greater glory of God, then we are the ones accomplishing (or failing to accomplish) his glory by our own effort—and that's just not something we can do. We are not the protagonists of history.

God's supreme glory is already present but often invisible or inaudible to his creation. But he engages us—the church—as antennae to resonate with the frequency of his glory and broadcast it to others. The antenna is not the hero of a radio or TV broadcast. But the antenna is important because it makes the invisible or silent frequency available to an audience. Our resonance with the glory of God is demonstrated by our joyful gratitude for him and his work. It showcases his grace and truth to the world.

This antenna metaphor for our participation in broadcasting God's glory illustrates the centrality of prayer in Christian leadership. In our prayer, we resonate with the frequency of God's glory. We place ourselves in dependence on the Holy Spirit and align our lives with his kingdom.

Let's take a wide-angle look at Jesus' life as portrayed by Luke. After Jesus' baptism, a pattern emerges in his leadership. He goes from action to prayer to action to prayer, like a song on repeat. Ronald Rolheiser notes:

> In [Luke's] Gospel there are more descriptions of Jesus in prayer than in all the other Gospels combined. Luke gives us glimpses of Jesus praying in virtually every kind of situation: he prays when he is joy filled; he prays when he is in agony; he prays with others around him; he prays when he is alone at night, withdrawn from all human contact. He prays high on a mountain, on a sacred place, and he prays on the level plane, where ordinary life happens. In Luke's Gospel, Jesus prays a lot.

Especially early in Luke's Gospel, the wilderness illustrates this pattern of prayer. As we saw in chapter three, the wilderness is the desolate place into which the word of the Lord speaks. Luke alludes to the broader biblical theme of God's people traveling in the liminal, transitional space between their old home of slavery and their future

home of complete salvation. The wilderness is also the social landscape of power, wealth, and identity, like John the Baptist's wilderness
of soldiers and tax collectors, rich and poor, Jewish and not (see
chapter three). The Spirit prepares the way for the Lord in the real
world of our society. Also, as we discussed in chapter six, character is
formed in the wilderness where Jesus goes to be tested by the devil.
Luke shows the wilderness from several angles. Like a diamond's
beauty, we see it differently from many angles.

But there's a common thread running through these wilderness
themes. The wilderness is always a place of prayer, and prayer functions in our lives much like the wilderness functions in the narrative
of Luke.

Luke makes it clear in his first two chapters that the word of the
Lord arrives not just in the wilderness but in an environment rich with
prayer. Before John the Baptist, the Hebrew people were waiting
around four hundred years for a prophet to speak the word to Israel.
Luke shows the word beginning to arrive when the angel Gabriel visits
Zechariah in 1:5-20, and the scene is all about prayer. Zechariah is a
priest, one called to represent the people before God and vice versa.
On this day he is chosen to serve by burning incense at the holy altar—
a Hebrew metaphor for the prayers of the people rising to God. Luke
notes that "when the time for the burning of incense came, all the
assembled worshipers were praying outside" (1:10). Everyone is
praying for Zechariah's prayers!

The angel reinforces this theme of abundant prayer. His name is
Gabriel, and he was last seen in Daniel 9 visiting a prophet known for
his life of prayer. Through metaphor, imagery, and direct reference,
Luke emphasizes that John the Baptist is arriving to Zechariah and
Elizabeth in a scene of abundant prayer. And in chapter 3 of Luke, the
word comes to John in the wilderness, after a thirty-year wait.

Jesus also arrives into a scene full of prayer. We see this in the faithfulness of Mary and Joseph and the worshipful response of the shepherds. We see it even more clearly when the baby Jesus is brought to

the temple in Luke 2. Two old saints of prayer are there in the temple waiting for him. Simeon is described as righteous and devout, waiting for the consolation of Israel and full of the Holy Spirit (Luke 2:25-27). He welcomes Jesus and offers a beautiful prayer of blessing and worship. In addition, Anna the prophet is in the temple waiting for Jesus. She is a very old person who has spent most of her life in the temple worshiping, praying, and fasting (Luke 2:36-38).

God calls disciples and leaders in the wilderness of prayer. In the heat of that wilderness, he forges his followers into people of prayer.

All Christians pray, but how does one become a person of prayer in a deep and comprehensive sense? It requires taking on prayer as a calling and an identity more than an activity. In my thirties I began to sense that I was called to be a praying person who leads rather than a leader who sometimes prays. God was calling me to make prayer my primary identity rather than action. He was leading me to act more like an antenna than an engine. During this decade my leadership stretch assignments came in developing intercessory prayer in Inter-Varsity nationally. I sought to spend enough of my leadership time in prayer that it might seem unwise to others—but if the leadership was fruitful, God would get the credit.

This meant that I needed to prioritize prayer and deprioritize some other things. Practically I decided to spend at least one hour in prayer every morning and let the rest of my schedule adjust around that commitment. I also decided I would say yes to every invitation or opportunity to pray with a group. At the time, I was supervising a gifted team of young missionaries. I loved that team! I realized with sadness that my focus on prayer would mean less time supervising and training my team.

I remember a conversation at the end of that year with Julien, who had previously been my student and now was directing the ministry on a campus. He shared with me that he was hurt and disappointed by the reduced time I had given him that year. It broke my heart to hear this, because Julien was (and still is!) dear to me. As we continued to discuss the year, however, Julien agreed that the fruit of God's work in his life and ministry was greater than the previous year. I shared with him that I, too, felt the cost of my prayer experiment that year—but I also felt the rewards in my growing relationship with God. Through costly prioritization, I was becoming more of a prayerful person.

Becoming a person of prayer also requires long experimentation and learning. Prayer is relational and therefore different for each person. Like any other relational effort, it takes practice and repetition, and it grows organically. In his book *Prayer*, Hans Urs von Balthasar makes the point that prayer is essentially dialogue, because God has communicated with us first. We begin by responding to his ever-expanding revelation in Christ. Von Balthasar notes that in this dialogue we must learn the language of God, which takes time and practice. We learn to speak and we learn to listen. Many Christians have briefly attempted to learn prayer. They try a particular formula or strategy, and like someone sucked in by a learn-a-language-quickly scheme, they give up early in the process. What a tragedy! For if we persist and practice, we begin to open the treasures of intimate communication with God.

Here is how von Balthasar describes the believer's breakthrough in learning prayer:

> All of a sudden we just know: prayer is a conversation in which God's word has the initiative and we, for the moment, can be nothing more than listeners. The essential thing is for us to hear God's word and discover from it how to respond to him. His word is the truth, opened up for us. . . . God's word is his invitation to us to be with him in the truth. We are in danger of drowning on the open sea, and God's word is the rope ladder thrown down to us so that we can climb up into the rescuing vessel. It is the carpet, rolled out toward us so that we can walk along it to the Father's throne.

Scripture is our reference point in the experience of hearing from God in prayer—but as we practice, we also learn the movements and communication of the Holy Spirit in and around us.

For me, the social process of learning prayer has lasted decades, and sometimes I feel like I'm still in the beginning stages. My early learning was formulaic and individual, following a scripted outline and lists of prayer requests. This helped me set some disciplines and begin to learn the grammar of prayer.

Other stages of learning have involved group prayer and learning from mentors. As with learning a language, prayer learning is social. We gain vocabulary and a deeper sense of meaning as we pray with others. In those years when I was saying yes to all group prayer opportunities, I encountered a *lot* of different kinds of prayer experiences! When prayer was available, I would always ask for it. When someone wanted prayer, I would always offer and initiate in that moment. When I learned about a prayer meeting, I would always go. Because I was curious about prayer and hungry for God, I gained something from every opportunity.

Some of those prayer experiences were awkward and many were foreign to my experience. I have found it especially enriching to learn from prayer cultures different from my own, so I have sought out prayer mentors from Eastern Orthodox, Catholic, and Pentecostal traditions. Some of my mentors have been friends, and others have been authors or speakers. I don't agree with everything I encounter, but I learn from everyone I engage.

In this journey I have found that some practices work well for others but not for me, and vice versa. I have also found that some practices work for me in different seasons of life. As I mentioned in chapter four, praying with Orthodox icons has been deeply transformative in certain periods of life, and Ignatian Gospel contemplation enriches my encounters with Scripture. However, I've tried some things that don't fit me. The Roman Catholic practice of praying the rosary is more robust than many assume. It leads to directed, prayerful reflection on particular themes and scenes in the life of Jesus. But the rosary has not been helpful to me, so I've moved on to other approaches. Sometimes I follow written devotional material, and in other seasons I pray out of my own pattern of Bible reading. I usually journal several times a week, but sometimes I take a break for a few months. My point is this: A deep life of prayer is profoundly important and satisfying—it is worth a lifetime of learning. And our learning changes organically, like a living relationship.

How does a life of prayer integrate with leading in the way of Jesus? Devotional prayer shapes our discipleship growth, and intercessory prayer shapes our leadership calling.

DISCIPLESHIP AND DEVOTIONAL PRAYER

God shapes the tender humility of our discipleship through all kinds of devotional prayer. I'm using *devotional* as a broad category to cover many practices of prayer. Being a disciple is like being a student or apprentice. Both students and apprentices require abundant communication—just as disciples require abundant prayer. In devotional prayer, we interact with God in ways that shape our life of following him. Sometimes devotional prayer is individual. My daily time of Bible study and prayer in the morning helps me grow as a disciple. My evening time of examen prayer increases my awareness of God's presence and movement in my life.

At other times devotional prayer is communal. For one semester in my college years, a group of about ten of us gathered five nights a week to practice listening prayer and learn by experience about the ministry of the Holy Spirit. God used that practice in community to form all of us. We grew as prayerful disciples because we learned from each other's experiences and not just individually. I also include healing prayer as a devotional practice. When we receive prayer for healing, comfort, or deliverance, God shapes us as disciples through the help of a caring friend.

Devotional prayer forms us at the deepest level of our being, ministering the themes of the baptism of Jesus to our souls. When we spend time in the Father's presence, we begin to hear his affirmation, "This is my beloved daughter or son, with whom I am well pleased." We receive God's affirmation of identity, affection, and pleasure as words spoken directly to us. This deep formation often happens through contemplative practices. Saint Teresa of Ávila describes multiple levels of contemplative prayer using the metaphor of water. In her autobiography she makes the point that the most basic level of prayer (which she describes as learning to get water from a well by using a bucket) is reflecting on the loving sacrifice of Jesus and gratefully receiving his love. In order to grow at this fundamental level, we must learn to receive love and listen to the voice of God.

We receive the formation of radical rest through devotional prayer as well. Sabbath, retreat, solitude, and silence are considered forms of apophatic prayer. Desert mothers and fathers used this Greek term to describe the spiritual practices of abstinence and silence. Kataphatic spirituality describes disciplines of engagement, but in apophatic prayer we enter the realms of silent waiting and the quieting of our hearts and minds. Silent waiting is an important kind of prayer. Even naps can be profoundly prayerful as we choose to trust God and rest. In sabbath we cease striving and expect to encounter God.

When we are in the testing of character formation, our devotional prayer most often involves engaging the Scriptures and our community around us. Jesus seemed to be feasting on Deuteronomy during his temptation in the wilderness, and his victories over temptation came directly from that text. It is the same for us—our devotional engagement with the Bible gives us clarity and strength to overcome temptation and grow in character. In times of testing I also depend on friends to speak the truth to me in love. God uses their perspective to shape my prayers and form my heart. Fasting is also an important devotional discipline for our character formation. Jesus shows the way by his own fasting in the wilderness of temptation. As we follow him in fasting of various kinds (abstaining from food is not always the right choice), we learn to depend more fully on God, who shapes our hearts and minds.

Finally, our various devotional prayer practices help us with discernment in our journey of personal formation. As we learn God's
language and the movements of the Holy Spirit, we begin to embody
wisdom for each moment. Our formation as disciples helps us to
choose well.

LEADERSHIP AND INTERCESSORY PRAYER

Prayer shapes our leadership journey as well. Our life of prayer is foundational to our leadership, just as Jesus' life of prayer was the foundation
of his leadership. Jesus was anointed by the Spirit and affirmed by the
Father at his baptism. He was sent by the Spirit to the wilderness for
testing, which he engaged by prayer and fasting. All of these happened
before he was clearly empowered and sent into Nazareth to announce
his calling. In the rest of his Gospel, Luke shows Jesus as a person of
prayer who leads rather than an activist who sometimes prays. In the
shape of his narrative, Luke gives the impression that prayer is where
Jesus gets the remarkable power and wisdom and love with which he
leads. Jesus seems to "pray his mission" as much as he "does" it. This
can be true for us as well.

We pray our leadership through intercession. The word *intercession*
means going between two parties as a mediator. A great mediator de-
velops intimate knowledge of both sides of a disagreement, builds trust
with both sides, and helps broker an agreement. So too with intercessory prayer: we mediate the tension between God's grace and truth
on one side and the broken earthly situation on the other. In prayer
we listen to God and we listen to the world. We feel the tension between holiness and sin, truth and deception, justice and injustice.
Feeling that tension, we "stand in the gap" (Ezekiel 22:30-31) as Moses
did when the Lord's anger burned against Israel (see Exodus 32:9-14).
We offer our earthly situation to God and ask him to act. We also offer
God's own words and character back to him and ask him to show
faithfulness to his covenant and purposes.

Let me acknowledge that intercessory prayer is mysterious and raises awkward questions. Here are some that come to mind:

- If God is sovereign, why should we get involved in the messy business of mediation?
- What difference does prayer actually make in the world?
- It is profoundly emotional to engage the tensions between God's will and human experience. How is it worthwhile? Why not leave it alone?

I can't answer any of those questions completely, as they all involve mystery. However, let me tell you why I am passionate about intercessory prayer and leadership.

First, I'm passionate because God invites leaders into his present work in the world. The Scriptures make the case that God is completely sovereign *and* the prayers of his people make a difference. In the example in Exodus 32, God changed his mind after Moses' intercession. I don't know if God planned beforehand to change his mind, but it seems significant that God involved Moses in his feelings and decisions about his people. In prayer, Moses understands and feels God's anger and his mercy. He understands God's perspective. When leaders intercede, God involves them deeply in his own feelings, thoughts, and movements in the world.

At least from our limited frame of reference, our prayers make a difference. I've been involved in Christian student conferences for close to forty years now, and my informal research has told me that an event surrounded by focused prayer is much more effective than one with little prayer. I can't prove that the prayers compel the Holy Spirit to move. I can only observe the difference. When a conference has a dedicated prayer team interceding before, during, and after the event, we see more conversions, healings, and transformations. With a prayer team, we also generally see ministers thriving more than they do during events without a prayer team.

Second, I'm passionate because intercessory prayer changes us. Out of his experience with God, Moses is described as the humblest man on earth (Numbers 12:3) and God's friend (Exodus 33:11). His intercession shaped him that way. In my experience, intercessory prayer draws me closer to God and makes me a better leader. When I bring the tensions of my leadership life into prayer, I pause to listen. "Lord, what do you feel about this situation? Lord, what do you see in this situation that I don't yet see?" Often when I pause this way, I find my mind drawn to a word from Scripture or a new perspective on the situation. Sometimes I gain a real sense of passion in praying a specific prayer because I realize the prayer resonates with the Holy Spirit's desire.

I recently went through a difficult season where our organization needed to restructure and multiple staff were laid off. It was painful, messy, and profoundly confusing to many people, and I met daily with both leaders and vulnerable employees. For several months I spent my morning prayer times in the Psalms, daily asking God for words of truth and comfort. Remarkably, every single day in that season I experienced the Lord providing a specific word of comfort or direction to someone through my morning psalms. In a time that was personally painful, God increased my faith, encouraged my heart, and empowered my leadership through intercession.

This kind of prayer is emotionally demanding, but the rewards make it worthwhile. In intercession I become more deeply involved in God's heart and action, both in the world and in me.

Our intentionality in leadership is important. We pursue a vision of influence or culture making, and God uses that in the world. When we look at our call to leadership from God's perspective, we see it in a new light. We see that God is involving us in his good work in the world. From this perspective, intercessory prayer is inherent to our call to lead. Leadership is one side of the coin and prayer is the other.

As Jesus prayed his mission, so we pray our leadership. Through our prayer and leadership, God involves us in his redemption of history. He also shapes us in the image of Jesus. Intercessory prayer tunes us to God's perspective as we read the social landscape around us. We observe our context through God's eyes, and we ask him to move. In intercessory prayer (as well as devotional prayer), God shapes our character and invests us with spiritual authority for the battle with evil in the world. Intercessory prayer is one way we engage in discernment of calling. We ask God for a direction, and then we look for signs from the Spirit to direct us along our pilgrimage.

Like Jesus, we as leaders are loved, formed, empowered, and called in the wilderness of prayer.

PRACTICE: GROUP INTERCESSORY PRAYER

There is no individual exercise for this chapter, only a group one. I'm convinced that prayer is best learned in community! So even if you're not going through the book with a group, I urge you to find a group with at least two others and try this intercessory prayer exercise.

GROUP GUIDE 6

EXERCISE: INTERCESSORY PRAYER (1 HOUR)

- Set aside time (I recommend an hour) and gather a small group to pray together—it's always better in community!
- Identify the tension you want to engage in prayer. The tension is usually a place where God's name is not hallowed or his kingdom is not obviously present.
- Spend time listening to God around these questions:
  - Lord, what do you feel and think about this situation?
  - Lord, what are you already doing in this area that you want us to recognize and encourage?
  - Lord, what do you want to do in this area, and how might we pray and act toward it?
- Record what each member of your group sensed or heard, and note any patterns. What Scriptures stand out? What words come to mind?
- Pray together in line with what you heard, especially any patterns and any Scriptures. Try to listen well to one another as you pray, and stay with a certain theme for a while before changing it.
- For the last five minutes of your prayer time, debrief your prayer experience together. What did you notice? What did you learn? What might God be calling you to do?

Note: For an inspiring, practical, and insightful exploration of intercessory prayer, see Carolyn Carney's *The Power of Group Prayer: How Intercession Transforms Us and the World* (Downer's Grove, IL: InterVarsity Press, 2022).

10

HUMILITY

Rehearsal for a Holy Death

Lord Jesus, we follow your lead in life and in death. Help us to consider our own mortality and, in doing so, to conform our journey of leadership to the image of your love and sacrifice. Like the grain of wheat that falls to the ground, please make our life and death fruitful in your kingdom.

What is your only comfort in life and in death?

That I am not my own, but I belong—body and soul, in life and in death—to my faithful Savior, Jesus Christ.

For five months of a sabbatical in 2007 and 2008, our family lived in Oaxaca, Mexico. We experienced crosscultural immersion together while I studied Latin American Christian spirituality. Abby and Gabe, in fifth and seventh grade, went to a local Mexican school. We engaged with church, art, music, neighborhood, and Little League baseball. To this day we often tell joyful stories of our time in Oaxaca.

In Mexico, the whole culture pauses and gathers with family on November 1 and 2 for Día de los Muertos. Even more than Thanksgiving in the United States, this holiday inspires travel and reunions across the country. Families remember and celebrate relatives who have died, and many build *altares*—displays with pictures of the deceased along with colorful decorations and mementos. Often a family will visit the cemetery to clean and decorate the grave, have a picnic with the late relative's favorite foods, and tell stories of their life. Those gatherings in the graveyard are associated with laughter and love. Many families also tell ghost stories—for example, how a certain dead uncle would always steal his favorite food or drink from the picnic.

That year we watched the city of Oaxaca pause its commerce, fill with beautiful decorations, and welcome extended family. All was focused on remembering the dead. Skulls and skeletons were everywhere, marked by vibrant colors and beautiful designs. Our son's baseball coach, Señor Blancas, graciously invited us to share his family meal of *mole de pollo*. The joyful focus on death felt awkward to me. I seldom visit graveyards, and I generally avoid thinking of death. I also felt a bit uneasy with the ghost stories.

Beyond stories of deceased uncle Oscar stealing the mezcal from the family picnic, people in Oaxaca would testify of encounters with saints and angels. Our friends and neighbors saw the world as a mix of the physical and spiritual. I remember an evening Bible study with friends from our church. We were sharing praises and prayer requests, and every person there (except me!) shared a story from the last week in which they narrowly escaped an accident or tragedy. Each one saw God's clear miraculous hand of deliverance. I realized I seldom perceive God's involvement in my circumstances. Instead, I tend to see science or even luck as the reason I made it through the day. I have often been blind to God's grace and real presence in my life.

In Oaxaca, my family entered into the local culture and learned (even a little bit) to remember the dead, tell stories, see more mystery in the world, and honor family.

DEATH IS IMPORTANT

Coming from a Western culture, I often need to be reminded that the world is more than my short life of concrete cause and effect. The Christian gospel gives us an animated view of history: God is involved in life and death through every generation, and God will bring all things to joyful completion. As the author and protagonist of history, God gives his people meaningful supporting roles that reflect his grace and truth to the creation around us. Even in death we are called to reflect his living triune image. The actions of life matter, but death also matters; it is more than just an end to our life in the body. Scripture encourages us to consider those who have gone before us in faith as a living cloud of witnesses, encouraging us to remain faithful in our own short lifetimes (Hebrews 11–12).

The center of our Christian story is one of death and resurrection. Every Gospel spends half of its precious ink and parchment on how Jesus died and rose again. To follow Jesus means we must contend with his entire journey. We are his disciples, and Jesus invites us to take up our cross and follow on the same journey he traveled, with a living awareness of our own mortality.

The action of Luke 3–4 takes place against a backdrop of death. John's ministry in the wilderness is not just an invitation to repentance. Rather, he claims that "the ax is already at the root of the trees, and every tree that does not produce good fruit will be cut down and thrown into the fire" (Luke 3:9). He invites us to imagine our demise as we consider the invitation to repent and be forgiven. John also introduces Jesus as the one who will "baptize you with the Holy Spirit and fire. His winnowing fork is in his hand to clear his threshing floor and to gather the wheat into his barn, but he will burn up the chaff with unquenchable fire" (Luke 3:16-17). John is doing life-and-death ministry. Our encounter with the word of the Lord in the wilderness is a life-and-death encounter.

As we saw in chapter five, the church has always seen the baptism of Jesus as multilayered. In addition to a deep affirmation of trinitarian love and completeness, the baptism is also a foreshadowing of Jesus' death. So too our baptisms become an enactment of joining Christ in the waters of his death and being raised with him to new life (see Romans 6:3-11). Jesus' genealogy emphasizes the passing of many generations and helps us remember ourselves in the legacy of mortal generations. The Spirit leads Jesus into the wilderness (a place of solitude and death) to be tested by the devil. In his forty days of fasting, Jesus goes to the limit of physical discipline and emerges victorious in spiritual power. So too for us—the shaping of our character affects the way we live and the way we die. Finally, even Jesus' active calling as he enters Nazareth happens under threat of his death. The people of Nazareth take him to the edge of a cliff to throw him off, but it is not his time yet (Luke 4:29-30).

So how might reflection on death help us grow as disciples and leaders?

DEATH, FREEDOM, AND JOY

Contemplation of death can give us the freedom to live in joyful embrace of our calling. When I lived in California, at the encouragement of my spiritual director Father Tom, I spent two days at an Eastern Orthodox monastery on a prayer retreat. I joined the monks in their regular prayer services five times a day and enjoyed their hospitality at meals and overnight. It was a fascinating crosscultural (or crosstraditional) experience for me!

The prayer services were long but also infused with passion and earnestness. Most of the liturgical prayers were sung or chanted, and there was a lot of body movement: bowing, crossing oneself, and kneeling. At one point everyone got in a single-file line to kiss an icon. I found myself curious, especially about the joyful, genuine faith of the brothers and of their abbot, Father Jonah. The community was poor, subsisting in large part on donations from the food bank in San Francisco. They sustained the monastery by making and selling two things: candles and coffins. They were especially pleased with the craftmanship of the coffins.

People chatted before coming to dinner, but when each meal began, the whole community entered silence and one brother read stories from an Orthodox book of martyrs. The stories all featured great faith and dramatic death. As I reflect on my experience of that retreat, two things that stand out to me are the joy of the community and their regular reflection on death. The coffins were a symbol representing beauty and mortality. And their community meals were a profound combination of life-sustaining nutrition and faith-inspiring sacrifice.

Giovanni di Pietro di Bernardone (1181–1226) was a wealthy and ambitious young man in his Italian hometown. By God's grace he became Saint Francis of Assisi. Francis's conversion and calling is a beautiful story told by dozens of authors over the centuries. The Holy Spirit clearly called Francis to follow Jesus in poverty and simplicity, to preach the gospel, and to lead others in joyful discipleship. Significant encounters with suffering and death mark the stages of Francis's transformation and calling. Different accounts of his life emphasize a variety of experiences, but all that I have seen include this pattern. Francis fought in a war in Perugia and spent a year as a captive. He was sick when he returned, and he began to sense God's calling on him. He went away for another war but lost interest and came home more committed to his spiritual calling. Francis had a transformative encounter with a leper, leading him toward a commitment to the poor and vulnerable. His central calling came from a mystical encounter with Jesus on the cross in the church of San Damiano near Assisi.

All these encounters with suffering and mortality seemed to direct Francis toward his calling but also to free him from captivity to wealth, reputation, and ambition. In a scene told by many biographers (and beautifully portrayed in the movie *Brother Sun, Sister Moon*), Francis is brought to trial before the Bishop of Assisi to account for how he is giving his family wealth away to the poor. In the town square before the bishop and a crowd, Francis takes off all his clothing, offers it back to his father, and walks off. Having encountered his own death, Francis is free to spend his life following Jesus' call. He lives in resurrection joy.

I had the privilege of getting to know Steve Hayner during the thirteen years he was president of InterVarsity. He was a man of towering intellect and impressive capacity, but those were not his re-markable gifts. He was not intimidating, even when he was the pres-ident and I was a student. Most impressively, he was joyful. Steve came to lead InterVarsity in a time when our movement was deeply divided, needing reconciliation and healing. A few years into his presidency, Steve began gathering groups of young leaders from different areas around the country. He brought fewer than twenty at a time so we could all fit in his living room. I remember entering one of those con-sultations, unsure if I could get along with many of the others. Somehow Steve's loving joy allowed us to speak our hearts and minds for several days and come out as friends. Several people from that consultation are my friends now, thirty years later.

One secret behind Steve's remarkable joy became clear in 2014 and 2015 as he navigated pancreatic cancer. Steve and his wife, Sharol (also a remarkable leader), chronicled their journey with cancer and death through daily reflections that were later assembled in the book *Joy in the Journey*. Steve's joy was resilient and contagious in part be-cause he had already counted the cost of his own death. Mark Lab-berton says in a foreword to the book, "Since his terminal diagnosis of pancreatic cancer during Easter week 2014, Steve's last nine months were like an advanced course in living and dying in faith, a story of honesty and hope. As he said, he had been training for this season his whole life, so perhaps it is no wonder that Steve did so well in the class! He would say it was simply a story of God's grace."

When I look at the lives of Saint Francis and Steve Hayner and the Orthodox monks from my retreat, I see disciples who experienced freedom and joy in part because they fully faced their own mortality. Having died with Jesus in baptism, they lived with him in resur-rection. Francis and Steve were not chained by the fear of death, and neither were they contained by self-absorbed arrogance. Humbled and inspired, they were able to give their lives more fully to following Jesus.

REHEARSAL FOR A HOLY DEATH

As we enter into Jesus' story, the church teaches us to rehearse our own death. Every time the church practices baptism, the whole congregation rehearses for both life and death. The ones being baptized are united with Christ in his death and raised to new life with him, and they also pledge themselves to live and die for Christ. The congregation witnesses these vows and also affirms its own life-and-death vows.

Every time we practice Holy Communion, we also rehearse for a holy death. We remember Jesus' broken body and his spilled blood, given in love for us—and we receive those gifts into our own bodies. The body and blood of Jesus then, on a spiritual level, make us one with him and with one another in his death across time and location. And so, as often as we practice Communion, we remember and rehearse our own death alongside Jesus.

This repeated rehearsal reminds us of the freedom and joy available to us. Without rehearsals and reminders, the voices of the world gradually take us captive. The world lures us to idolatry of youth and fear of death, but when we take up our cross, we remember both death and resurrection. We follow Jesus believing that through our reflection of his story, empowered by his Spirit, the whole cosmos is being redeemed. We also take up our cross believing that in our following we will become more like him.

This "rehearsal for death" version of Christian growth may seem intense or macabre to some, but it has been the vision of our discipleship for millennia. Our faith is not an individual improvement program in a materialist-functionalist view of the world. Rather, our growth is participation in God's expansive story bringing all of human history into worshipful alignment under Jesus. As we cooperate with the Holy Spirit, our life and death matter in God's scheme for the cosmos.

DEATH AND LEADERSHIP

What does this understanding of death have to say to our leadership journey? One might imagine that a whole-life vision of leadership would encourage caution or moderation, like pacing for a marathon rather than a sprint. This is true only in part. A life-and-death vision of discipleship helps us consider sustainable patterns for long-term growth in character and spirituality. Because I want to live and die faithfully, I will prioritize disciplines of spiritual, physical, and emotional health. However, considering life and death in leadership will also embolden our approach to taking risks in faith. Our call to discipleship and leadership is a call to take up our cross and give our whole lives. When we are reconciled to our death, we can be more free to joyfully risk our lives (or the world's vision of our lives) for the sake of God's kingdom.

In my decades of work with young missionaries in their twenties and thirties, I've noticed a few things about those who grow to become great leaders. Typically, those who are fruitful leaders later in life have rehearsed early for the most challenging parts. They have practiced losing their lives for the gospel. They have experienced failure and learned from it. They have learned to engage and navigate the most difficult conflicts. They have suffered losses and learned to grieve. They know how to repent and apologize. They own the blessings and sins of their culture and community. They have given away something precious to them, which usually forces them to start anew. These are all forms of rehearsing a holy death. Our leadership posture of tender humility and bold faith is possible only when we truly trust the death and resurrection of Jesus—and we learn trust through practice.

Ronald Rolheiser, in his book *The Passion and the Cross*, has helped me understand another angle on death and leadership. He makes the point that the passion narratives are not so much about what Jesus did but rather what was done to him. The first half of each Gospel is mainly what Jesus did and said—and it's wonderful! But the second half is about how he received the actions of others. The passive, receptive elements of Jesus' suffering and death are significant. The way we receive what is done to us is as important as what we do actively in the world.

If God is indeed the protagonist of history and we are supporting cast, then our heroic deeds and achievements are not as important as we might imagine. Many leaders ultimately fail despite their overwhelming commitment to leadership programs and projects and results. Some fail in character because they have neglected the inner work of healing and formation. Some fail spiritually because their ego becomes more and more important while their worship cools. Still others burn out, lacking the hope and joy to remain steadfast and resilient. When leaders fail, it breaks our hearts and often damages the redemptive influence they have had.

On the other hand, when leaders are faithful for a lifetime, the impact is enormous. Those who lead well *and* suffer faithfully demonstrate great spiritual authority: "Precious in the sight of the LORD / is the death of his faithful servants" (Psalm 116:15).

Leadership is difficult and the world is cruel. We live, and we will all die. As in any performance, the rehearsal pays off at showtime. Having practiced again and again for a holy death, we are better equipped to walk the narrow path of tender humility and bold faith and reject the slippery slopes of arrogance and fear on either side. Remembering that we have died with Christ, we are more free to live in his resurrection life. With the freedom gained from embracing our mortality, we become faithful and joyful in what we do and in what is done to us.

As the Heidelberg Catechism reminds us, we are not our own, but we belong—body and soul, in life and in death—to our faithful Savior, Jesus Christ.

PRACTICE: PRAY WITH PSALM 90

Begin by reading the whole text of Psalm 90, slowly. Note what stands out to you. Pray briefly in response to your first impressions.

Movement 1: Worship. Read Psalm 90:1-2 and worship God for the ways he has been faithful to his people through all generations. Note any ways God has been a shelter in your own life, and give thanks.

Movement 2: Mortality. Read Psalm 90:3-13. Spend time in prayer, recognizing and admitting the shortness of your life. Remember that you will pass away like every generation. Ask the Lord to speak to you about your mortality and limitations. Listen and note what you hear from the Lord.

Movement 3: Consecration. Read Psalm 90:14-17. Holding your sense of mortality before the Lord, ask for his mercy in all the ways you most need it. Ask the Lord to establish his beauty, pleasure, and favor in the midst of our finite generation. Offer your discipleship growth to the Lord. Offer your leadership—the work of your hands—to the Lord. Return to worship the Lord who is sufficient for every generation.

GROUP GUIDE 7

DISCUSSION QUESTIONS FOR
CHAPTERS 9–10 (30 MINUTES)

Prayer

1. What are your deepest desires for your personal prayer life?

2. What do you as a group or team desire for your prayer life together?

3. What would it take, as a person or a group, to gain that kind of prayer life?

4. Share one significant experience you have had with devotional prayer.

5. Reflect back on your experience of the intercessory prayer exercise at the end of chapter nine. What, if any, impact has that experience had on your group? How might a regular intercessory practice affect your group's culture or strategy?

Death

6. This chapter encourages you to contemplate your own mortality. What feelings does this bring up in you?

7. What might increase your freedom and joy as a disciple and leader?

8. As a group or team, consider the "mortality" of your group or organization. How might that help your group engage with freedom and joy in the present?

9. What might it look like for you, both individually and as a group, to regularly rehearse for a holy death? What difference might that rehearsal make for you?

OVERALL REFLECTIONS ON *FORMED TO LEAD* (30 MINUTES)

Individually

10. What overall impression are you carrying from reading this book?

11. What insights or convictions from Scripture discussed in this book have impacted you?

12. What is the central invitation you have received from the Spirit, and how will you respond?

As a group

13. What overall impression are you carrying from reading this book as a team?

14. What insights or convictions from Scripture have impacted you as a group?

15. What is the central invitation you have together received from the Spirit, and how will you respond?

GRATITUDES

I'M GRATEFUL FOR THE TENDER MERCY OF GOD, who has given all of the stories and any valuable insights herein. Any faults or wrongs are purely my own, and you have my apologies. Discernment, creativity, and communication are fundamentally communal, and others have carried me through the process. I've received feedback from a wide circle, including Abby, Gabe, Roxanne, and Dan Jensen; Jason Gaboury; Andrew Ginsberg; Dan and Jackie Bergmann; Bora Reed; and Bruce Hansen.

Christ Church Madison has been home and family to me in the writing, and Father Scott Cunningham has inspired many insights and convictions herein. Three superheroes have read every word of multiple drafts and given detailed feedback. Those three are Bobby Gross, Jim Herriott, and my amazing wife, Susi Jensen. What a wonderful gift it is to hear honest, smart, caring feedback and correction from people I love and respect! I'm supremely grateful and indebted to them for the improvements.

Susi has provided inspiration, patience, accountability, and steady love throughout the long process. Her superior writing skills have brought more beauty and craft to this book. Cindy Bunch and Rachel O'Connor with InterVarsity Press have been wonderfully helpful with editorial feedback and encouragement.

To all those who have led me, followed me, and led with me in the mission of InterVarsity, I thank God for you.

GROUP LEADER'S GUIDE

I'M SO GLAD YOU ARE GATHERING a group or team to process *Formed to Lead*! I believe that the group process will provide two great values. First, it will help each individual to go deeper with the content from Scripture and the book. Second, the group process will allow you as a group or team to process formation and calling on a communal level. These leader instructions will help your group get the most out of the experience.

1. *Facilitate.* You don't need to control. Your role as the leader is simply to facilitate the process. You don't need to be the team leader—anyone on a team or in a group can facilitate this process. The book and the questions will do most of the leadership work, so you don't need to direct or control.

2. *You don't need special preparation.* If you read the chapters, do the exercises, and are ready to engage the questions, you are ready to facilitate the group. If you want to spend extra time in the Bible studies and exercises, please do so—but it's not necessary for facilitating the group.

3. *Keep the calendar.* As the leader, you set the dates and times when the group can meet. Based on how quickly the group can read the chapters, choose whether the meetings will be weekly, monthly, or somewhere in between. I recommend weekly, since the chapters are relatively short. It helps to set dates for all seven group meetings at the beginning. Then if there are changes, you can just tweak one of the meetings. It helps to send a message to the whole group one to three days before the next meeting with a reminder of the chapters to be read before the meeting.

4. ***Keep the clock.*** Each group guide suggest time allocations, for example, thirty-five minutes for Bible study and twenty-five minutes for discussion. Your role as leader is to keep the group on time, discussing the questions offered. Sometimes it helps to tell the group, "I'm going to be the time keeper, moving us along from one thing to the next. Of course we can choose together to change the timeline, but unless we do that, I'll keep us moving along."

5. ***Stick with the questions offered (mostly).*** The questions in each group guide are designed to elicit a great discussion, so feel free to follow them verbatim. Of course, if a tweak or a different question fits the context of your group better, go ahead with that. And if you or the group sense the Holy Spirit highlighting a change, always go with the Holy Spirit's lead! But sticking with the questions offered will usually work well.

6. ***Pay attention to group dynamics.*** You may need to act as a shepherd for the group dynamics to help keep everyone engaged with the content and with each other. My first step in this is to pray for the group and to lead the group in praying for their community process. These group guides are mostly not "prayer meetings" (except for the intercession one), so I don't recommend spending a lot of time in prayer, but it helps to open by praying together for an excellent process. After that, keep track of whether anyone is dominating the group dynamic and if anyone is silent or less engaged. Sometimes it is important to specifically invite quiet people to contribute their thoughts. If someone is regularly dominating the discussion, it is usually helpful to address them privately, asking them to make more space for others.

NOTES

INTRODUCTION

2   *"Spiritual formation is a process"*: M. Robert Mulholland Jr., *Invitation to a Journey: A Roadmap for Spiritual Formation*, exp. Ruth Haley Barton (Downer's Grove, IL: InterVarsity Press, 2016), 16.

1. LEADERSHIP INTEGRITY

10   *Andy Crouch's thinking*: See three books from Andy Crouch: *Culture Making* (Downers Grove, IL: InterVarsity Press, 2013), *Playing God* (Downers Grove, IL: InterVarsity Press, 2013), and *Strong and Weak* (Downers Grove, IL: InterVarsity Press, 2016).

15   *Navigating this narrow path*: For a thorough treatment of Christian discernment, see Elizabeth Liebert, *The Way of Discernment: Spiritual Practices for Decision Making* (Louisville: Westminster John Knox, 2008). See also chapters 8 and 9 in this book!

2. ENCOUNTER

28   *Henri Nouwen summarizes*: Henri Nouwen, *The Way of the Heart: Desert Spirituality and Contemporary Ministry* (New York: Harper Collins, 1981).

29   *"God's call is mysterious"*: Carlo Carretto, *Letters from the Desert*, anniversary edition (Maryknoll, NY: Orbis Books, 2002 [1972]), xv.

3. CONTEXT MATTERS

38   *"God's preferential option"*: Pedro Arrupe, *Essential Writings*, ed. Kevin Burke, Modern Spiritual Masters Series, ed. Robert Ellsberg (Maryknoll, NY: Orbis, 2004).

4. FORMATION

48   *"The river Jordan"*: Found in *The Festal Menaion* of the Orthodox Church, in the Liturgy of the Baptism of the Lord.

50   *"The main thing"*: Stephen R. Covey, *First Things First* (New York: Simon and Schuster, 1994), 75.

5. RADICAL REST

58   *Lidell was considered*: For a great article on the history and context, see Greg
     McKevitt, "'It's Complete Surrender'—Olympics Hero Eric Liddell and the
     True Story Behind Chariots of Fire," BBC, July 8, 2024, https://www.bbc
     .com/culture/article/20240705-olympics-hero-eric-liddell-and-the-real
     -story-behind-chariots-of-fire.

59   *Sabbath keeping is revolutionary*: See Walter Brueggemann, *Sabbath as Re-
     sistance: Saying NO to the Culture of Now*, rev. ed. (Louisville: Westminster
     John Knox, 2017).
     I'm indebted to Eugene Peterson: Eugene Peterson, "The Pastor's Sabbath,"
     Christianity Today, May 19, 2004, https://www.christianitytoday.com
     /2004/05/pastors-sabbath.

64   *"The man who is wise"*: Referenced at "Are You a Reservoir or a Canal?,"
     Unhurried Living (blog), August 16, 2016, https://www.unhurriedliving
     .com/blog/reservoir-leadership-tool.

6. CHARACTER FORMATION

72   *The parallel with the exodus story*: Moses' message from God, and his
     message to Pharaoh, was to let the people of Israel go into the wilderness
     specifically for worship. See Exodus 3:12, 18; 4:21-23; 5:1.

73   *In these reflections*: Henri Nouwen, *In the Name of Jesus: Reflections on
     Christian Leadership* (New York: Crossroad Publishing, 1993).

75   *Henri Nouwen reads this*: Nouwen, *In the Name of Jesus*, 35.

78   *Fasting, solitude, and silence*: For additional context on these disciplines, see
     Adele Ahlberg Calhoun, *The Spiritual Disciplines Handbook: Practices that
     Transform Us* (Downers Grove, IL: InterVarsity Press, 2015).

80   *I was in my midthirties*: Every three years, InterVarsity Christian Fel-
     lowship hosts this North American conference focused on mobilizing each
     generation of college students to give their whole lives for God's global
     purposes.

7. LEADERSHIP CALLING

90   *Luke shows that the Holy Spirit*: For a profound and comprehensive
     treatment of this, see Rainero Cantalamessa, *The Holy Spirit in the Life of
     Jesus: The Mystery of Christ's Baptism* (Collegeville, MN: Liturgical
     Press, 1994).

96   *Carlo Carretto's story*: Carlo Carretto, *Letters from the Desert*, trans. Rose
     Mary Hancock (New York: Orbis, 2002 [1972]).

98   *In fact, he names his memoir*: Eugene H. Peterson, *The Pastor: A Memoir* (New York: Harper Collins, 2011).

     Winn Collier's excellent recent biography: Winn Collier, *A Burning in My Bones* (Colorado Springs: WaterBrook, 2021).

102   *I am indebted*: See Gordon T. Smith, *Beginning Well: Christian Conversion and Authentic Transformation* (Downers Grove, IL: InterVarsity Press, 2001).

8. CYCLES OF DISCERNMENT

109   *"The Desert Fathers believed"*: Thomas Merton, *Thoughts in Solitude* (New York: Farrar, Straus and Giroux, 1999).

117   *I offer . . . more resources*: For a good starter on Ignatian discernment see James Martin, *The Jesuit Guide to Almost Everything* (New York: HarperOne, 2012). For a deeper dive see Gordon T. Smith: *The Voice of Jesus: Discernment, Prayer, and the Witness of the Spirit* (Downers Grove, IL: InterVarsity Press, 2003).

118   *"Practicing a preference"*: Stephen A. Macchia, *The Discerning Life: An Invitation to Notice God in Everything* (Grand Rapids, MI: Zondervan, 2022), 14.

     Another preliminary practice: See Elizabeth Liebert, *The Way of Discernment* (Louisville: Westminster John Knox, 2008), for more guidance on shaping the question.

9. PRAYER AS LEADERSHIP

127   *"In [Luke's] Gospel"*: Ronald Rolheiser, *Sacred Fire: A Vision for a Deeper Human and Christian Maturity* (New York: Image, 2014).

130   *In his book* Prayer: Hans Urs von Balthasar, *Prayer*, trans. Graham Harrison (San Francisco: Ignatius Press, 1986 [1955]), 14-15.

     "All of a sudden": von Balthasar, 15.

133   *In her autobiography*: Teresa of Ávila, *The Life of Teresa of Jesus: The Autobiography of Teresa of Ávila,* trans. E. Allison Peers (New York: Image, 2004).

10. HUMILITY

139   *"What is your only comfort"*: From the Heidelberg Catechism. See "Heidelberg Catechism," Christian Reformed Church, https://www.crcna.org/welcome/beliefs/confessions/heidelberg-catechism.

144   *One secret behind*: Steve and Sharol Hayner, *Joy in the Journey: Finding Abundance in the Shadow of Death* (Downers Grove, IL: InterVarsity Press, 2015).

     "Since his terminal diagnosis": Mark Labberton, foreword to Hayner, *Joy*, 16.

145　*The church practices baptism*: For an example of baptism liturgy from my Anglican tradition, see "Concerning Holy Baptism" in the Book of Common Prayer, 2019, https://bcp2019.anglicanchurch.net/wp-content/uploads/2019/08/22-Holy-Baptism.pdf.

　　The body and blood of Jesus: Depending on your theological and ecclesial tradition, they may make us one with him more concretely and literally, but all Christians can agree on the Eucharist emphasizing our spiritual union with Christ and one another.

146　*Ronald Rolheiser, in his book*: Ronald Rolheiser, *The Passion and the Cross* (Cincinnati: Franciscan Media, 2015).

⟨⟩ IVP formatio

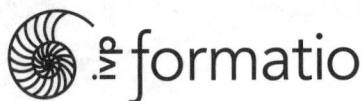

The nautilus is one of the sea's oldest creatures. Beginning with a tight center, its remarkable growth pattern can be seen in the ever-enlarging chambers that spiral outward. The nautilus in the IVP Formatio logo symbolizes deep inward work of spiritual formation that begins rooted in our souls and then opens to the world as we experience spiritual transformation. The shell takes on a stunning pearlized appearance as it ages and forms in much the same way as the souls of those who devote themselves to spiritual practice. Formatio books draw on the ancient wisdom of the saints and the early church as well as the rich resources of Scripture, applying tradition to the needs of contemporary life and practice.

Within each of us is a longing to be in God's presence. Formatio books call us into our deepest desires and help us to become our true selves in the light of God's grace.

LIKE THIS BOOK?

Scan the code to discover more content like this!

Get on IVP's email list to receive special offers, exclusive book news, and thoughtful content from your favorite authors on topics you care about.

IVPRESS.COM/BOOK-QR